WOODWORKING FOR BEGINNERS

Helping New Woodworkers Make Better Projects

(The Complete Guide to Help You Create Easy Woodworking Projects)

Peggy Valdes

Published By Zoe Lawson

Peggy Valdes

All Rights Reserved

Woodworking for Beginners: Helping New Woodworkers Make Better Projects (The Complete Guide to Help You Create Easy Woodworking Projects)

ISBN 978-1-77485-249-1

All rights reserved. No part of this guide may be reproduced in any form without permission in writing from the publisher except in the case of brief quotations embodied in critical articles or reviews.

Legal & Disclaimer

The information contained in this book is not designed to replace or take the place of any form of medicine or professional medical advice. The information in this book has been provided for educational and entertainment purposes only.

The information contained in this book has been compiled from sources deemed reliable, and it is accurate to the best of the Author's knowledge; however, the Author cannot guarantee its accuracy and validity and cannot be held liable for any errors or omissions. Changes are periodically made to this book. You must consult your doctor or get professional medical advice before using any of the suggested remedies, techniques, or information in this book.

Upon using the information contained in this book, you agree to hold harmless the Author from and against any damages, costs, and expenses, including any legal fees potentially resulting from the application of any of the information provided by this guide. This disclaimer applies to any damages or injury caused by the use and application, whether directly or indirectly, of any advice or information presented, whether for breach of contract, tort, negligence, personal injury, criminal intent, or under any other cause of action.

You agree to accept all risks of using the information presented inside this book. You need to consult a professional medical practitioner in order to ensure you are both able and healthy enough to participate in this program.

TABLE OF CONTENTS

INTRODUCTION 1

CHAPTER 1: THE REASONS TO USE HAND TOOLS 6

CHAPTER 2: SOME OF THE BEST PATIO PROJECTS 24

CHAPTER 3: WOODWORKING PROJECTS 34

CHAPTER 4: STARTER TOOLKIT 40

CHAPTER 5: A LOOK AT THE WOODWORKING ROUTER AND ITS SUPPORTING TOOLS 58

CHAPTER 6: WHAT IS THE BEST WAY TO MILL A BOARD TO MAKE FOUR SIDES SQUARE 75

CHAPTER 7: SELECTING THE WOOD TO MAKE USE OF 80

CHAPTER 8: SELECTING THE BEST WOOD TO USE 91

CHAPTER 9: WOODWORKING TIPS AND TECHNIQUES... 101

CHAPTER 10: DIFFERENT KINDS OF WOOD 114

CHAPTER 11: WHAT TO MAINTAIN WOODWORKING TOOLS 131

CHAPTER 12: CHOOSING THE RIGHT TOOLS FOR THE JOB 142

CHAPTER 13: MODERN WOODWORKING TOOLS OF TODAY 151

CHAPTER 14: SHOP SAFETY 161

CHAPTER 15: WOODWORKING HAND TOOLS AND MACHINERY 167

CONCLUSION... 181

Introduction

Woodworking is a craft that has existed for a long time in the history of mankind. The great thing about woodworking is that you don't need to be doing it on a an all-time on a regular basis. It is possible to work part-time and also take part in other business activities.

When you've learned how to construct wooden objects and tools, you can make an amazing present for the special person to you. It is not necessary to purchase an expensive present to your spouse or acquaintance. You could make them something special and make them feel appreciated and valued.

You could also make use of your woodworking abilities to earn some cash by commercializing the idea. For instance, you could begin to make furniture and sell it for profits. You could also begin cutting wood to meet the specifications of the customer.

It's a great hobby to take up. Woodworking is among the most enjoyable hobbies because it can keep you entertained and will help you turn your creativity to use. In addition it's a low-cost and enjoyable hobby.

Are you aware that you can completely transform your house and enhance its value by using wood products? All you need to do is learn how to build wood products and you'll be good to go. You can, for instance, create a unique dining table that can completely change the interior of your home. It is also possible to build an impressive chopping board that will impress your guests once they lay their eyes at it for the first time.

Researchers from all over the globe have estimated that it will take less than 10 seconds for a person who you have just met to make first impressions of the person you are. If you're considering expanding your business and bringing with more clients You must put an individual appearance in your workplace. For that, you need to create a unique and appealing piece of furniture, and place it on your desk. When a new customer enters the office space, they'll get an impression of you and thus increase the chances of completing the deal. What type of client would be hesitant to do business with an individual, well-organized and tidy person? Furniture will show you as a highly clean, organized and focused person.

Ever thought about having a unique piece of furniture which isn't found anywhere else. If you want to stand out from your peers, colleagues and coworkers You can choose to create something with wood. For instance, you could create an effigy of you as well as your dog.

What should you do if you purchase an 42-inch television, while the most powerful wall unit on the market is able to accommodate 24 inches of TV? There's no need to be concerned. You can always construct the wall unit if are skilled enough to build it. If you have woodworking skills, you are able to build something that's not readily available on the market.

Furniture of high quality is expensive and can cost you money. While you'll require longer, but it's less expensive to build your own furniture. Therefore, you should consider building instead of purchasing furniture.

If you are able to master woodworking and are proficient in woodworking, you will never need to hire carpenters to fix damaged furniture. Repair the broken furniture by replacing broken piece or by repairing it.

There is no need to purchase plastic furniture if you are unable to afford furniture made of wood. Wood furniture is attractive and helps a house or office appear more natural. Another drawback of plastic items is that they're not robust. When you master how to work with wood, you are able to make furniture for your office or home.

The skills you learn from woodworking will bring you joy and increase confidence in yourself. You'll feel much more confident when you can point to an item of furniture that is within your home and inform your guest that you're the person who designed it.

Chapter 1: The Reasons to Use Hand Tools

Utilizing hand tools is a lot easier than mastering the hand skills to use the keyboard of a computer. I should know that -I'm not able to type an ounce (even having been a certified journalist) and I've learned to use chisels, rasps, planes, hammers and braces with minimal effort. This is because I've learned that using hand tools isn't just an issue of manual dexterity. It's not about acquiring organic gifts. It's not about years of gruelling training. It's more than having an apprentice with an internal master who can steer the way. It's more about overcoming an obstacle that blocks the majority of living

different kinds of wood

Employees: the stress of placing a bet and then mucking up the work you're doing by searching for a fresh approach. I see this all the time with woodworkers. If we have successes with

remarkable performance, we then aren't looking for a innovative method to perform this procedure, as it seems to be risky. In addition, since the majority of people (although some) have heard about the art of power sources (through magazine, store courses or even television) and that's what we're accustomed to.

Hand Tools: The Myths of Hand Tools

There are some woodworkers who have no reason to play with hand tools. We have these extremely fast and precise power tools available to us. Why is it that people "devolve" into a former scientific state? This is

a bit contrary to our ingenuous way of thinking. The reason you should incorporate hand tools into your work is because almost everything you hear about hand equipment could be wrong. Let's an examination of some of the misconceptions.

Myth #1: Employed machines aren't fast. The truth is that a lot of people are sluggish. Hand tools were designed to be

It is imperative to get the job done as quickly as it is can be. It is all about getting them set up and properly used. It is important to choose the appropriate tool for the job. It is not advisable to reduce a plank's depth by using an sanding block. And why would you want to achieve this feat with a jet

Are you using eroplane? The programs all are slow when

Inappropriate. About seven decades ago when we had editors from our woodworking magazine line

The idea was to come up with an identity for the baby he was born to. It was an idea for a small idea

He did however spend three entire hours planning all the wood for the job on the Delta 13" cast-iron industrial planer. What's the reason? Because he was unable to get rid of more than 1/16" during a turn. He was afraid that it would cause damage. The truth is that the hand and power tools can be quite fast if set up properly and used correctly. It is important to know that an airplane is used to the purpose of slicing off 1/16" of material at one stroke. It is essential to understand that a hand with 7 points can fly through an unfinished plank with half the amount of strokes you would have to make with the 12-point saw. It is important to know that a cabinet saw can form wood faster than the standard patter.

Nmaker's rasp. When you've mastered the basics, you're likely to increase your rate.

Myth 2 The idea that employed tools are less precise than tools. If I hear someone is laughing, I ask the person whether they can use their table saw to take .001" from the border of a board. It's almost impossible to accomplish using an ordinary table saw router jointer, or planer. But

It's fun for children to learn how to use a plane. After a day of practice

Sing using a handplane, then you'll be able to use any handplane to remove shaving cream that is .001"-thick shaving cream.

Imagine the energy you can get from. Pruning and trimming your muscles can be easy

Once you have that skill. It's a straightforward capability to attain.

Hands-on tools let you free of these unrelated measurements. The doorway panels don't matter if they're. 0625" thick or .061".

The only thing they are concerned about is whether they are in line with the stiles and rails. If you cut the wrong size plank to be able to slide on a table saw you'll be caught in a never-ending sequence of trimming, visiting the seat, check the fit, alter the design, clip and then visit the seat to examine the match. You must then smooth the board to complete. If you match a board with a hand plane you can put all of it on the floor. Just take a few steps to evaluate the match, take several moves, then verify the match. This is the actual pointer. After it is found you don't have to sand the hand plane genera

It is a surface that is ready to be finished. This means you're more efficient and more precise.

Myth 3 Hand equipment requires skilled use. A lot of people believe that when using hand tools, requires years of instruction to master this instrument. While a precise control of any instrument (hand or motor) is unlikely but many hand-tools can be discovered within only a couple of minutes (not several years) of learning. Go to the shop and decide to try out scraps of wood. Stir it, cli

p it, plane it, form it, split it. If you've achieved anything you can

Apply these abilities in your job. It is a second aspect of information that has been lost and will help to dispel this myth about hand tools: people believe they can be used exclusively freehand. It's not true. There is a range of straightforward "appliances" or jigs which can allow you to direct your hand gear. Shooting boards aid to plan perfect straight edges and finish boards. Bench hooks help you maintain and guide your work when using the backsaw. Sawbenches assist in making your handsaw perform well through the work. Stops to planing are a way of removing complicated tools for holding. Making some of these devices will reveal the hidden capabilities of your hand equipment.

Myth 4: Basic hand tools are not suitable for difficult work. In reality, we have an impressive array of shop-made and industrial electrical tools jigs today. There are dovetail jigs that are more costly as my old pickup. Belie me, modern jigs can are able to do the job. I've used a number of these. I think the jigs are so popular because some woodworkers are awed by gadgets (nothing wrong with that) and some woodworkers think they need an elaborate jig in order to carry the task such as cutting out a mortise and tenon joint. Hand tools generally free you from the complexities of jaggery. Consider for a moment how difficult it can be to remove an chemical mit

Re-shape the table saw, particularly on the board. There's a huge amount of test cutting and installation involved. There are tons of sample bits that have been wasted. Also, i

If you really want to cut it right it is recommended to buy an aftermarket mitre estimate which is accurate to a half-level. If I want to cut an unusual angle, I mark it on my workpiece, and then only cut through the lines. After that, a few strokes with a plane , wash the cut, and then I ensure that it is exactly the same. No evaluation cuts.

A waste of substance. No jigs. Mark the line; cut along the line.

It's among the most liberating emotions you'll ever have. It's not difficult to accomplish.

Myth #5: Employed equipment are less expensive than electrical tools: "I bet you didn't expect me to talk about that. Great tools for the price. It's a good price. It's over. This is because that you can buy classic hand-tools or old machines for a lower initial cost. However, ensuring that these tools work properly can make a huge difference in the amount of energy and time. If you have a good amount of time to spare and enjoy playing with metallic objects, that's the best option for you. For those who believe who time is scarce Get the finest tool you could. You will end getting it sharper by it by using it for longer. This has been the case decades ago. In Joseph Moxon's Mechanick Exercises of 1678, the author encourages novices to buy high-quality steel gears instead of the iron gears that are less expensive and also specifies exactly where they can go they can go to London at Foster Street to receive them. Nearly every outdated book about woodworking I've got says you must

Always make sure to buy the highest quality that you can afford. Audels Carpenters and Builders Guide (Audel Co. 1947) says so:"(I)t is

important to buy only the best, regardless of cost." When I was a kid my first with an Craftsman. Some of the resources available from Craftsman are

There are many who are. This was a piece of a mess. The knife clamp was never functional. The framework buckled during normal use. The handle that was riveted was loose. The mechanism that controlled the blade's angle was often loosened. The majority of the stuff I've observed has been a shambles. So it's not a surprise that I found

Ght is a problem using this specific tool. I have finally found a nice Olson Saw Co...

The management was watched. The day I began with that, I saw my sewing abilities improve by ten-fold. Affordabl

The tools can be a hindrance in the way of working. High-quality tools make the job easier than it could be.

How do I begin?

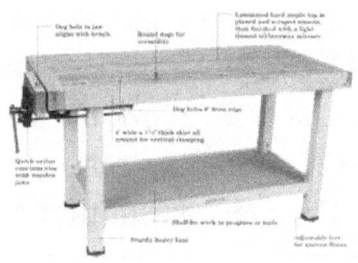

If this sounds appealing to you, you're likely to be wondering where to begin. The first step would be to get yourself educated on the materials prior to purchasing them and making use of them. Although there is a lot of sound advice on this subject it is recommended to read to read a few books to help you find the essential information you need. I have several favorite books on hand woodworking. There should be at least two one on sharpening and the gear. I would consider buying the

Sharpening your pencils with e-books. There are only two novels that I love for sharpening: The Complete Guide to Sharpening by Leonard Lee, and The Complete Illustrated Guide to Sharpening by Thomas Lie-Nielsen. Both books are published by The Taunton Press, and both will guide you through the basic steps needed to sharpen a variety of tools. For a quick overview the hand tool and the applications they have Below are some excellent sources to look through the library and in the bookstore. the library (a couple of these books are no longer available, but are still useful within libraries).

Hand Gear by Aldren A. Watson (Norton). Although Watson is a boatbuilder with a narrow viewpoint, his beautiful hand gear examples are worth the price of gold. This book is affordable and easily accessible, as well as packed with information that you'll refer to regularly.

Traditional Woodworking Tools are available from Graham Blackburn (Blackburn Books). The first casting book I owned was written by Blackburn. The book incorporates many of the columns published in publications in the past several years into the form of a

An excellent reference book for the job.

Programs for Woodwork by Charles H. Hayward (Drake). Unfortunately this

The book that is enjoyable is no longer available in the market. Hayward examines the tools are needed to master woodworking.

Restoring, Tuning, and Utilizing Classic Woodworking Tools by Michael Dunbar (Sterling). If you're planning to follow the route of repair

If you want to have the best tools, then are going to want this book. It's a bit difficult to locate however it's worth the effort.

The Workbench Book by Scott Landis (Taunton). You'll need a great workbench to perform hand functions Landis's work is timeless. Avoid imitations. This is the way to go.

The perfect book for seats available. After that you'll need an inventory from Astragal Press, that specializes in publishing and selling books about well-known crafts. You'll find a number of fantastic books that guide you through the avenues which you're interested in, for instance hand planes, dentures, or saws

There is no reason to reject electricity.

There's one last thing I'd like to say concerning hand gear. Utilizing them shouldn't cause you to disbelieve in machines or tools. Many people who visit my home-based store are awestruck by my eight" Powermatic jointer, Delta Unisaw, and the Grizzly 15" planer. "I thought you were an expert in hand tools," would be the unavoidable comment that comes from your lips. I'll then mention the number of braces that are disgustingly large hanging from the ceiling behind the group saw, and in addition, the hand planes that are kept in a cabinet made of cherry on top of my grandmother's work bench. "I am a fan of all of the tools," is my typical answer. Hand tools and power tools work in a modern workshop. Both viewpoints complement each other in a variety of ways, allowing workers to work more quickly and more precisely, with less waste, and more enjoyment. It is possible to mix the two perspectives according to your desires.

I use my power planer and jointer to prep my extensive inventory, however the hands' tools handle all of the last truing , and also create the pieces of work that are ready to finish. I use my tablesaw to cut and rip (its function in the first place) and also use my own hands' tools to complete nearly all the top joinery. The work is overseen by the tools I have in my shop and the top quality work is accomplished through the hands' gear. What I have learned from my experience with the power of hand tools and also the power of it is that I'm an expert woodworker.

Innovative tools, projects and methods are a good chance to be attainable when you have a range of ways of doing a particular task. If I have to wait or get annoyed at the task ahead of me, I remind myself that I should behave more like an 8 year old boy.

Chapter 2: Some of the Best Patio Projects

The patio is an ideal location where homeowners can unwind and unwind. It's out in the open, surrounded by the natural surroundings and fresh air that could do you a whole lot of good. The only issue is where to be seated? This chapter will attempt to solve that problem by presenting some of the finest furniture for patio projects.

Backyard Couch

The backyard and the couch should be connected to tranquility. What if we tried for ways to connect these two sources of rest and relaxation by making the backyard couch? Then, you've got it! Since this woodworking task gives you the perfect spot to put your feet up to enjoy a relaxing afternoon in the sun!

For starting out, you are likely to require a few tools, and these are:

Router

Nail Gun

Kreg Jig

Sander

Square

Multi-Square

Drill

Miter Saw

Measurement Tape Measurer

To get started, you'll need cut pieces that will be your side pieces first. In order to do that, take out your kreg jig , and alter the settings until it's placed at 1 1/2 inches. The next step is to drill a few "pocket holes" in the edges of the wood, so that you can connect the whole thing together. Once you've done this, you will then be able to fashion the parts that make up the upper portion of the structure.

After this is done it is now time to begin drilling these "mitered" edges. The leg-boards should be glued into the assembly. After that, put all the components in their respective places and then glue them in place. Then, you'll be able to make the boards that make up your seat.

Attach your seat slats to each other in the structure by screwing them into place. Then, cut out the components that create your sofa's armrests. Join them to the frame using glue and woodworking screws. Take the pieces which will form the back slats and join these to the rear of your couch. The backyard couch is now complete!

Patio Easy Chair

The only thing that is easier than making this chair is sitting on it! All you need is one or two 1 4s, some 2 x 4s, and an old-fashioned 2 x 2, and you're ready to go! Start by taking two x 4s and cut into half. Then, use them to create your arm rests and legs. Then, take your 2x 2 . Use the base to where you can attach your arm and leg rests.

Utilize wood screws to secure the assembly. Set your 1x4's up on the base and make diagonal holes in the standing wood and into the base. After that, connect the wood and base. This is what will make the seat of your chair. You can then make use of the rest of the wood to make the back of your chairs , leaving about one-half inch between each of the components. It's the complete Patio Easy Chair! Easy enough, right?

Deck Bench

A deck bench can be an essential part of any patio decoration. In order to begin you will be required to build the base frame for your bench. This means that you'll be required to design your bench from 2x4

sections of wooden. To make this happen, you need to take out two 2x4's and make use of a band saw to cut into two pieces. Set these two pieces on top of each other and secure using woodworking glue.

Take another piece of wood and design your arms and legs from it , too. Make holes in those legs' tops and connect these to your bases using screws for woodworking. The same drills can be made into the sections that form the arms and then screw them into the same way. For a final touch you can use the power jointer to eliminate all rough edges.

Patio Garden Box

The garden box on your patio is a wonderful location to set your flower arrangements. Before you start the most crucial thing you have to be able to determine the space you're going to require to accommodate your flowers. Also, you should be aware of the amount of outdoor space you may have.In other terms, how large are your outdoor space? After these questions are answered , you are now able to proceed with making arrangements for the Patio Garden Box installed.

Take your boards and cut them through the middle. Then, you can put the entire thing together in a rectangular form. The Patio Garden Box is ready to start. Add soil, seeds and water and you're good to go.

Patio Porch Swing

When it starts to get warmer and people start to take a walk soon, people begin to set their sights at a swing set to use on their outdoor patio. To begin, you're going to need to build the basic frame that resembles a window.

It can be accomplished with two 2 x 4's as well as four 1 2's. Set the 2 x 4's parallel to each other . Starting from the top to fill them evenly with the 1 2's. Attach them by screwing them together to keep the structure in position. This is the base part of the porch swing.

Next , you need to cut a length of timber and make an arm rest on the opposite side. Then, you can create the back of the chair, and then add some cushioning.

Then, take two hooks made of metal and secure them to one corner of your back of the swing. Then, chain them up onto the porch's ceiling. Make sure that it is solid and sturdy, and your porch swing will be ready roll and rock!

Patio Stool

It's a basic but essential furniture piece for your outdoor patio - the outdoor stool. The stool is comprised of the primary structure that you are sitting on, the legs that stand up and bracers. Begin by taking the wood in its raw form and making your 4-inch bracers to form on the side of your stool. You will then need to build what will be the legs, as well as your backing structure , which will connect the structure to your bracers. This is the frame for your stool.

Now that you've got this information, you can begin filling in on the sides of your frame using the appropriate size wooden panels. Make holes in each panel as well as the supporting structure, and then join the entire structure by using wooden screws. When the structure is put together it's the matter of aesthetics. If you prefer more rustic style take your chair in its current configuration.

However, if you're looking for to give your patio a more polished look, make use of your jointer with power to smooth out all rough edges. Then, apply some woodworking varnish and your patio stool is now ready to go. There you go you guys--the very most beautiful patio work!

Chapter 3: Woodworking Projects

The most effective way to improve your woodworking skills is to begin by working on basic projects. Many skilled woodworkers began their careers humble but over time, they developed additional skills that allowed them to tackle bigger projects until they reached the point where they are today. Begin slow and build your skills while you build more projects. This section provides a number of easy projects you can begin with. Always use protective clothing and tools while doing any work regardless of how small. In this way, you'll not get injured during the course of your work.

Simple wooden boxes

Select the wood you want to use. When you are starting your first project you could make use of wood or a piece of a previous project which is no longer needed or purchase and cut fresh wood. The kind of wood you select is determined by the purpose of the box once the project is completed. For instance, thinner wood is ideal for smaller boxes since it is easier to handle and cut.

Make sure you have all the materials you'll require. The tools you'll need to complete any project must be at hand in your workspace. At a minimum, you will require nails, a hammer adhesive, putty, and finally, your wood. If you plan to use an electric tool it is essential to make sure that you're close to an electrical source.

Make sure you mark your boards. It is important to do this in keeping the dimensions of your box with an eye on the size of your box. Find out how long, wide and tall your box is likely to be before you draw the markings on your boards with an ruler or pencil.

If the boards aren't in the correct dimensions, cut them into sizes. A circular or hand saw is suitable to do this. The power tools could make the job more simple, but they're not essential in this particular project.

Put the pieces by using an adhesive butt joint. Begin by joining the two sides at right angles with the adhesive you prefer. Then, hammer or drill the finishing nail onto the sides. Wood screws are a good choice or dowels as well.

Attach the base of the container to its sides. Make sure that the sides are perfectly on the baseand then apply an adhesive to secure the sides to each other. After it's dry you can then hammer into nails to finish the box.

Connect it to its lid, making it complete and useable. The lid that is hinged the ideal choice for an wooden box. In order to put it on you must set your box's lid against its side in a smooth way. Draw out the places where you believe the hinge is needed. Now, you'll be able to drill the hinge with nails and a hammer. Make sure that the knuckle on the hinge is facing away towards the back of the box.

This box has been made finished. You can improve its look by putting some finishing to the surface. If you have nail holes you can fill them with wood putty. Once the putty is dry you can sand the surface to smooth.

A Tiny House

A tiny, wooden home is an ideal task for the novice woodworker. It could put as a bird table, or even as an decorative, provided you have a idea in mind with the proper tools and equipment to complete the task. This is a step-by-step guide that will assist you in building an usable wooden home to begin your first woodworking project:

Create an foundation for your home. This is done by excavating the land where your house will be situated. For a tiny home it is only necessary to have an area of a few square feet, so the area won't be huge.

Place boards all over the foundation with the exception of the portion that will be the place where the door will sit. These boards will be the walls of your house.

Make sure that you fill the foundations of your home in order to make sure that the boards remain straight and do not wobble.

Keep your boards in close proximity. It is possible to do this by hammering nails on small pieces of wood that is placed between each wood piece that is on the wall. You can put tiny pieces of wood on the walls of your home to ensure that the walls are joined. Make sure that the wall is sturdy enough to support the wall, and then cover the nail holes to cover the nail's ends.

Install a roof on your home. It can be accomplished with the large piece of wood capable of covering the entire house between one end and the next. Set the wood over one of the wall panels in your home and then join the roof board and wall to each other. Make the boards in the amount you require for the ability to cover your entire home.

Design an entrance. Hinged doors are the best alternative. Choose a piece of wood that will fit perfectly in the opening left for the door. Set it up against the wall, and mark the area for the location where the hinge is. Install the hinge on the door, then put the other hinge against the wall. Examine to confirm that the door opens and closes without difficulty.

Chapter 4: Starter Toolkit

If you decide to take on woodworking, your first step is to acquire all the tools that you'll require. In the majority of cases you'll already have the majority of most basic tools in your house. However, it could be wise to buy a few additional items of equipment. You may also wish to upgrade some of the items in your tools, to make certain that you have the right set prior to beginning to work.

In any event there are two major types of tools that you should be aware of hand equipment and electric tools. We will take a look at each one along with a list of the most essential tools you should be equipped with from each. We will also look at some of the tools as well at some of the other tools you could include in your toolbox shop.

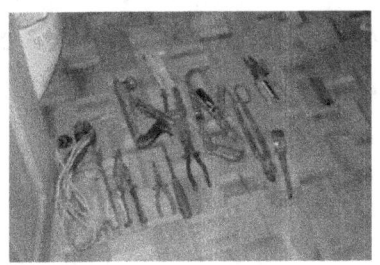

Hand Tools

A variety of hand tools

Hand tools are the simplest to find when you are starting your woodworking since they are easily available at house and are affordable. Here are a few indispensable hand tools that a standard woodworking kit must consist of.

1. Hammer

The claw hammer is the most well-known of woodworking tools. It allows you to insert nails into pieces of wood but also remove them with it's clawed ends. The clawed end can also serve as a counterweight that keeps the hammerhead in balance. It is also handy for many other purposes.

The weight is a crucial factor when buying Hammers. A heavier head means more force per stroke, making driving a nail more effortless. But, it can also make it a bit more difficult to manage. Another crucial aspect to consider when buying an hammer is its handle's size. The longer handles, the quicker you can swing the hammer more force. The weight that is most popular for the claw hammer is 350 grams.

2. Hand saw

The hand saw is a different hand tool almost always related to woodworking. And , despite the advent of power tools, such as the jigsaw and circular saw, a lot of experienced woodworkers consider it essential to have at minimum two hand saws in their toolbox.

RIP SAW

SAW CROSSCUT

There are many types of handsaws that are available, the two most important types to include in your starting set are the rip as well as the crosscut saw. The primary difference between the two saws is the way they cut through the wood as the ripsaw cuts across the grain, while the crosscut slices across it. Additionally, how many teeth (denoted as teeth per inch/tpi) will determine which saw should be used to cut an exact amount of lumber. Saws with higher tpi can be used to smaller wood stock, whereas smaller tpi are suitable for cutting more aggressively on larger pieces.

If you don't want to carry around two equipment, you could opt to buy a saw that comes with interchangeable blades.

3. Tape Measure

A RETRACTABLE MEASURE TAPE

It is vital to be precise when working on a wood-based project because you need each piece to conform to the specifications to ensure a perfect fitting. For this is where a tape measure will be better than an ruler because it's much smaller and is easy to carry around when needed. A retractable tape measure that is 25 feet would be the best choice, as any length greater than that could make the retract mechanism not function properly.

When you purchase your tape measurement It is crucial to verify the strength of the hook that is at the end. If the hook is loose, it could slip out of position and throw off your measurements as far as one 8/8 of an inch that can affect the accuracy of the measurement by a significant amount. Be careful not to let the tape slide back too far so as to not harm the tab.

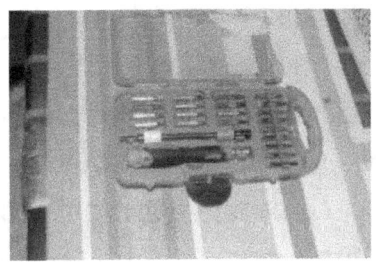

4. Screwdriver

Screwdriver set that can be interchanged with bits. The bits are standard sizes used in everyday use.

Screws can be useful for when you need to quickly take apart the pieces that are joined. However, they can also be quite an inconvenience in the absence of the correct size screwdriver for the task. A great set of screwdrivers should contain the most commonly used size that are suitable for Philips or flat-head screws. Although it isn't as common is the case, it's beneficial to have some top drivers as well as Torx drivers for these screws.

5. Chisel

The chisel is likely to be one of the least well-known of the hand tools used by the majority since it is frequently used for carving wood. The chisel could actually be a useful piece because it is able to be used to clean joints or saw cuts. Additionally, it can be utilized for such unique tasks as removing two pieces of wood from each another.

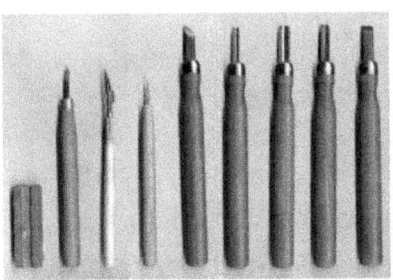

A COLLECTION WOODWORKING CHILDS

When you purchase chisels it's an ideal idea to purchase various sizes. Select chisels made of high-carbon alloy steel or chromium-vanadium steel, which are resistant to wear and tear for a longer period of time. Make sure to get wooden grips and caps of metal at the edges, as this will withstand hammer strikes with ease.

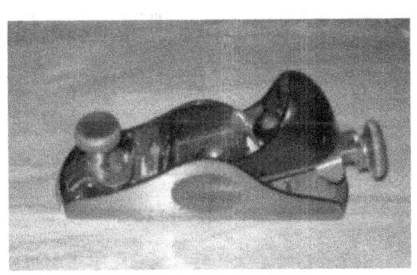

6. Hand Plane

PLANE BLOCK PLANE

Although the hand plane is often neglected by newbies however, it is one of the tools essential to an initial kit of woodworking tools must have since it is not just used to smooth wood, but also to shape it to suit your needs and trimming it in order to meet the required measurements. Block planes are an ideal starting point for those who are new to the field. You're likely to be amazed to find out that buying older block planes is beneficial, since metal used to make the components is usually higher.

Power Tools

Power tools are made to make woodworking tasks completed faster and less difficult. They come in two varieties of corded tools, in which they require plugging into the power outlet or cordless tools, which come with their own battery packs. Nearly all power tools come equipped with a variety of attachmentsthat allow them to perform the tasks of a variety of different tools.

1. Circular Saw

Although the circular saw can be thought of as more of a tool for carpentry but it is also indispensable to the woodworker's craft. The circular saw allows woodworkers make cuts that are able to be saw. It can also be used to cut precisely by clamps that hold the material that is perfect for working with wood or fiberboard.

Similar to the handsaw, the amount of teeth is essential when selecting circular saws as well as a saw blade. A blade that has more teeth makes more precise cuts, which are perfect for cutting precise cuts.

2. Jig saw

Cutting curves in wood is not an easy task to complete using standard saws. Jig saws make the job easier because it gives greater control over the cutting direction. One thing you'll want to include in the jig saw is an orbital action. As opposed to conventional jig saws that simply move the blade upwards in a downward and upward direction, orbital Jig saws tilt the blade to the forward, to drive it into wood during the upswing to create a more smooth cut.

Be aware the fact that these features are generally preferred in the more expensive models however, you can still find it

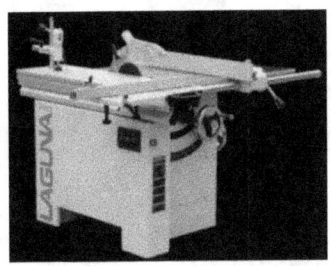

3. Table Saw

For the majority of beginners who are just starting out, the table saw will be the first purchase for their shop. Because it's where the majority of the work focused. Table saws allow you to chop large chunks of wood and can also accurately reduce smaller pieces to the desired size. Table saws are often equipped with components that allow you to cut different thicknesses of wood at angles you prefer.

4. Power Drill

Cutting, then drilling holes is another typical task you'll be faced with. You'll be amazed to learn that a power drill with a cord is a better choice than a cordless drill. This is because corded drills are more affordable and are able to keep power on for a longer period of time.

5. Router

The router is a multi-faceted tool that novices can use to complete a range of tasks. An stationary router is a great choice for those who are just starting out, since it will allow you to get the most work accomplished quickly. Pick a machine that's more than 2 horsepower higher with enough capacity to handle larger pieces.

6. Random Orbital Sander

RANDOM ORBITAL SANDER WITH SANDING DISKS

In all woodworking activities Sanding is the most tedious since you'll spend hours attempting to get the desired level of smoothness on the wood's surface. Random orbital sander helps make the task easier and also frees your hands of the burden of having to rub sandpaper over the wood. Another advantage of this type of sander the fact that it minimizes the look of visible scratch marks caused by sanding because it is moving in a random manner instead of a distinct pattern.

Tools, tools and Items

Apart from the tools above in addition, there are a variety of other tools you need in your toolbox. These tools will serve you well to accomplish a range of tasks and could also be utilized when you need some tools that you can't find.

1. Clamps

Clamps are among the most essential items in the shops. They are used for everything from holding glue-bonded pieces securely together while the glue is forming as well as holding the pieces that are being cut, or securing the bent wood beam to form. Clamps come in a assortment of designs, including spring clamps, bar clamps, face clamps corner clamps as well as C clamps.

2. Pliers

While pliers are usually used in electronic and electric work, they have many uses in the shop. Similar to clamps, pliers can also be employed to support wood items during work. Pliers are also used as a wrench that can be used to loosen bolts from wooden panels, and also as a lever to pry wood pieces.

3. Levels

When creating items such as cabinets and tables It is essential that they are level on the floor. A level can be helpful to determine if it is the situation. A standard level is an incredibly clear cylinder that is filled with liquid there is a bubble inside.

4. Speed Square and Builder's Square

The speed square can be described as a device that lets the woodworker know whether the parts that have to be in right angles to one another are actually such. The most basic of this is simply an L-shaped ruler.

5. Marking Tools

The two most commonly used marking tools you need to keep in the workshop are chalk and the carpenter's pen. The chalk is your standard kind that is easily purchased at school supply shops.

6. Work Stations

Workstands are particularly helpful for people who need to work in tiny space. They are a great way to store the tools you're using so that they don't end up floating all over. Work stands are also extremely useful when you need to move from one area to another. You can prop them wherever you're required to.

7. Air Compressor

The majority of power tools that you have are powered by electricity. But, there are some that are powered by compressed air for instance, the pneumatic nail gun. But air compressors are far more efficient than running pneumatic tools because they can also be utilized to power various other tools.

8. Vacuum Cleaner

A thing to be aware of when working with wood is that it's going to be extremely dusty. Therefore, you will require an efficient vacuum cleaner to get rid of dust after the work. But, ordinary vacuum cleaners have not been designed to handle huge amounts of sawdust.

Chapter 5: A Look at the Woodworking Router And Its Supporting Tools

A Woodworking Router is a standard instrument used in the wood industry. They are very popular with staircase designers and pattern makers because simple, intricate designs made of wood are simple to design. It was also getting more popular in the cabinet business because it was useful for a variety of reasons.

Before the boom of power tools hand tools included a massive hand plane of wood with an elongated blade that protruded from the plate that was used as the base. This type of design was known as "Old Woman's Teeth" due to its resemblance in shape. Woodworkers continued to develop their products due to its many advantages.

Despite the advent of modern motorized tools old-fashioned device was still in use by woodworkers and carpenters. The need for greater technological advancement led to the introduction electronic routers. This has opened the way to the development of the various routers available today. This is a look at the most modern tools available today.

Different types of Routers

A woodworking router is typically available in two main kinds: the handheld and the table that is mounted. The dimensions of your plan is contingent on the equipment you choose to. Table-mounted equipment is equipped with an additional worktable. This is a great option when you are creating smaller, delicate pieces as they are easier to manipulate. The bits of a router face upwards and let you cut your pieces with greater precision. They are also saferas the wood components are secured and secure. It's the ideal option when you're just starting out or working as an individual woodworker instead of being a professional.

Handheld devices typically come with large handles, with the motor located at the center with the handle on both sides. The locations of these components are designed to make movement more manageable. It allows the most user-friendly control and control on the equipment. Certain models are new and do not include features that were present in earlier models. The most well-known models is dust collection systems that eliminates the sawdust. It's especially impressive when you don't have the right workshop to work in for your work.

Pieces and router bits come in a variety of sizes and shapes. Every diameter type produces diverse effects on wood or other materials using which you work. Half-inch pieces are a popular illustration for hobbyists and professionals.

They are strong and create smoother cuts. They are also less susceptible to vibration , too. The handling is less unstable and allows you to design patterns quickly.

Certain online stores make specific router bits designed to fulfill your cutting needs. These tools are great when working with smaller-sized materials or for such delicate tasks as restoration. Take a look at these tools if your work involves the use of the original mouldings and woodwork trims that are no longer readily available.

Get your work-router and the bits. Think about the things you are planning to make or repair prior to looking at the choices. Ask for advice from carpenters contractors, or even personnel from the hardware business to determine the best solution for your needs. There are risks associated when using woodworking routers. It is essential to buy appropriate protective equipment, such as safety glasses, gloves, and pillows. These products will help protect you from harm when you begin the work.

The router bit for woodworking and woodworking are the ideal tools for modern-day homeowners

Do you want to could create a work of art using wood? Are you in need of a little assistance in completing repairs to wooden items? Have you thought about the use of machines with these projects? If you've answered 'yes to all of us, then you ought to think about purchasing woodworking routers and bits in the near future.

What is a good wooden router?

It is a tool that is used to make various shapes and designs in wood. The machine is usually employed to create structures on the edges of wooden panels or to hollow out its center.

The router we have in the present is just a remnant of the tool it used to be. The router was it was a hand-tool made of a wide, wood hand plane, with a narrow blade that is distinct from its base plate prior to the time that electrically powered machines became readily available. The distinctive look of the router gained its elegance "Old woman's tooth" from the woodworking people and capitals.

In those days the patternmakers and workers for staircases used woodworking routers. They were extremely useful as they were able to create basic designs that were complex. Cabinet manufacturers also favored to use these tools because they were beneficial to the field. The designs that were developed showcased a meticulous artistic style and attracted many customers to purchase cabinets and other items with elaborate designs.

Even though electronic equipment was already in the marketplace, this device was still in use. A lot of workers and manufacturers were able to attest to its value and used it until increased production was needed. This led eventually to the development of electronic machines in United States and other industrial nations.

What are the different kinds?

There are two kinds of tools that are available currently: (1) handheld and (2) table routers. Handheld buttons are typically put in the middle of the machine, or on one handle. The device typically features two handles on each side and an engine in the middle. This feature allows users control the machine. The person using it will be able to glide easily and control movements by shaping or cutting wood.

Table routers are worktable-mounted machines. They are often used to create smaller pieces that require more details in design. Many wood artists and amateurs frequently cite their value in this regard since it offers precision cutting. It is also useful for novices because the wood used is held securely.

What are the parts that make up the router?

Router bits are devices designed to work with routers. They are available in a variety of sizes and shapes with distinct purposes. Straight bits can be used to make horizontal or straight cuts. It also helps to hollow wood. A lot of employees have also praised their effectiveness in removing material in small increments, when connected to a special router.

Why should I own these instruments?

If you are looking to complete DIY wooden projects then buying is an option. You can also repair or repair wooden furniture, cabinets and more, with the right tools and techniques.

It's simple to purchase woodworking routers and other bits on the Internet. Make sure you read the customer and business reviews which are offered at fair costs by online vendors.

Simple tips to purchase Woodworking Routers and Bits

Woodworking isn't easy but it are also rewarding. Because of your expertise and patience, you will be able to begin working on small projects , and even repairs. There are some things you should be aware of about routers, bits and routers for woodworking.

Types and functions of woodwork routers are able to help make, design and repair furniture made of wood. Its functions permit users to create designs that are easy to cut, cut, and reproduce patterns that are already in place. It was utilized for a long time as wood was used by people for centuries.

The woodworking router was once able to operate manually, but nowadays it runs on electric power. There are a variety of fixed-base, dip trim, and combo router kits to choose from.

Plunge routers are equipped with an engine that is attached to the base that is loaded with springs. It is the most secure kind, since users are able to use it to hold the wood. The ability to plunge can contribute to the result safely and precisely. There are many versions that include 1.75 horsepower (hp) and 100 volts capability.

Fixed-base models can range from 1.75 or 3 hp.and you can make use of it by lifting or lowering the engine's base. This is the easiest kind of engine for students to utilize.

With the help of enthusiasts and carpenters wood is cut across. The machine is extremely precise as it is able to cut to micro-cm.

Trim routers are less hefty, often known as laminate routers. The maximum capacity of this device is one horsepower or less, and it became a huge hit because it's easier to use. Due to its size and simplicity of use the user can use it after a proper education with just one hand. This tool is perfect for laminated surfaces since it is able to provide accurate cuts.

Combo woodworking models consist of a medium-sized machine that has a fixed base as well as a plunge base. Combining the best characteristics of a plunge and fixed router, it's as if you bought two tools. The greatest thing about it is that it provides the same features as bases are used with table-mounted or handheld models.

Pieces and router bits are the attachments to the woodworking router. Every bit is available in various dimensions and shapes with various applications. Straight bits, for instance vertical and horizontal cutting tools. They are perfect if the solid wood is hollowed or cut into.

Attachments that flush cut require cutting bits. These tools include a pilot of the same size as the cutting radius. The bearing acts as an effective guide, and it can make different shapes that are identical when employed in patterns.

How do I buy

The router needs experience and requires a thorough evaluation. For novices, it's simpler to utilize the fixed base router. You can learn to use the machine with amount of time, and with practice. This is suggested for projects that are simpler.

The purchase of router bits is offered in sets. They can be as large as 15 12, 7 and 8-bit packagesthat come in different sizes and functions. Find out what bits are included before you decide to purchase one package over another. Certain sets have vital parts like straight trim and the flush trim, while others have more intricate models.

What is a router and how it can be utilized.

I'd suggest looking at the word"router" before as it comes from the verb rout, which means to go. Routing can also be a noun however, it doesn't relate to the woodworking router we use. It implies that the meaning behind the word is similar to an instrument, a tool or a device. Maybe my idea of the term "woodworking router" is to weight the piece of wood or to grind it. It could be just an opening or a rounding of the edge of the piece wood.

They were powered manually and shaped as the flat plane of wood, however, they were equipped with small, adjustable blades instead of the large flat blade. The blades were shaped to create an edging or a grove of the wooden. In the beginning of the century an electronic router was invented however it was a different product that could achieve the same findings . It was built on a spin cutter and was referred to for its spindle-shaped router. The first products were created by a company known as Elu and I recall using an Elu router that was of high-quality. I believe Elu is now an integral part of Makita's Power Tool and Makita's product line.

The first electric routers were fixed-base, and later routers were called plunging routers to stop the spinning blade from protruding over the bottom as the pressure or weight was taken away. The routers have been transported over woods. Another method is to set the router at the bottom of the table. After that, move the wood onto the router. Then, place the table router in an upright place. This is perfect for workshops and comes with additional safety features.

Handheld plunging routers that come with various controls can be utilized (should be utilized). The base of the router may be equipped with a sidebar so that the blade remains at an equal separation from the edges of the piece of wood that you cut. For example, the groove could be 4 mm in depth and 3 millimeters from the edge of the piece of wood. The width can be increased to a maximum of 4 millimeters, and the guide for the side assures it is formed by cutting the edges of the wood no more than 3 millimeters. The same result can be obtained by clamping a straight edge on the machining surface of wood, and then placing the electric router securely to the left.

Router cutters, also known as router bits come in various shapes and sizes. It is possible to use your router to cut square, vee and round grooves in various forms. There are more router bits available for round, corner and even decorative finishing of edges. A router has an incline that spins at the lower part of the cutter which keeps it from cutting the wood further. The purchase of router bits are usually a bit of a risk, as you're looking for the finest bits but don't want to invest the money. I suggest buying a variety of router pieces that come in all designs you could think of using, unless you require the most extensive range of router bits to do professional use. It is likely that you will require two or three straight bits. You may also need to shell out a bit more for if you intend to frequently use these bits to get the top quality is within your budget. It is possible for example to purchase a 3-4 mm straight cutting blade that is suited for the edges and groves of the wood you have chosen. A larger 8-10 mm is ideal for removing the wood from a bigger area. Blades that are less expensive will lose their cutting edge very quickly and could squat, or even melt the timer unless you take care.

A router from a variety of manufacturers is possible from the following brands: Makita, Bosch, Dewalt, Festool, Milwaukee and Porter-Cable. The router is an electric power tool that is cabled and is typically required for extended periods of time, which is why there aren't many routers that are cordless. This Ryobi ZRP600 Trim Router is an 18v cordless router that was specifically designed to allow for more comfortable trimming. A lot of manufacturers offer retrofitted routers as well as combination router kits.

Once you are able to master the use of a router, you'll be amazed at how many jobs that a router can help with.

Chapter 6: What is the best way to Mill A Board To Make Four Sides Square

The chapters prior to this point covered the basic tools you must use for your first time woodworker, and the various choices you can make regarding what tools to buy This chapter will explore a specific project you can complete. This is described as the process of milling a board to make it square on four sides. The chapter will not only guide you through the precise method of milling a piece of wood but it will also explain the term milling and explain the proper way to do it.

What does it mean for you to Mill Wood?

Milling wood is the process of taking the lumber piece and transform it into something smooth and square which can be later utilized to construct furniture. If the main reason you picked up this book was that you were trying to design furniture in the near future it is likely to be interesting for you. If a wood board is milled properly every face of the board are likely to be smooth and flat and all corners will measure precisely ninety degrees. This generally means that there will be six sides you'll have to mill. Let's examine the steps you'll need to take to cut the boards into squares with four sides.

Step 1: Make use of an a jointer

It's beneficial that we've previously discussed how to correctly use a jointer, as you'll likely require a jointer as the initial stage of milling your board four-square. If you're milling an object of wood be sure to get a 90-degree angle for all 6 sides. You may also check to ensure all angles have precisely ninety degrees after cutting the boards by taking measurements against the the joint's fence which is designed at a ninety degree angle. Another method to test to ensure that your sides are perfectly flat is to place them on an even surface. If the entire surface of the board rests on the surface completely If it does, then there is a level, level surface in your hands.

Step 2: Make Use of Your Block Plane

If you're still not convinced in the purchase of the jointer, you have options to mill your boards four-square. It is possible to use the block plane hand tool to accomplish the same purpose. Although this tool typically used to create an incline that is sloping on the other part of wood. However, you'll first need press the portion of the wood you would like to flatten to flat surfaces. If you observe an uneven or wobbling, those are the areas of your wood board that you are certain to remove. After you've marked the sections of your board which are uneven, you can apply the block plane and apply it until the board is flat and flat to the surface it is sitting on.

Step 3 Step 3: Find an Organizer

If you are sure that all edges of the board is level The following step would be to put the baby through the planer. We haven't discussed the use of a planer, but it is utilized to create a certain thickness across the entire board. It is vital that all sides of your board are smooth prior to running the surface through the machine. If there are edges of your board which have bows or concave inwards, the planer will duplicate these patterns and the board is likely look like a mangled mess. Since a planer isn't an essential tool for woodworking according to this book, the best option is to rent one at your local hardware shop or ask whether the hardware store is willing to plan the wood for you for a nominal cost.

Step 4: Return back to Table Saw

The final stage needed to mill a four-square is to complete the job using the table saw (or in our instance the circular saw). The circular saw is used to make sure that all the thin edges of this board remain perpendicular to and in line with one another and vice versa. If you follow the steps properly, your piece should look like something that follows similar to the one you see below. In the image it might appear that it's relatively easy to build a board that looks like this, however you could consider taking this for granted since you're used to buying good wood from the market. We hope that this article has given you a glimpse of the process required to create a well-managed board that is then used for shelving or as a practice mechanism after the board is coated with varnish.

Chapter 7: Selecting the Wood to Make Use of

In order to give your work the look you want just any wood will not suffice. It must be the right type of wood that fits your taste. Similar to meat in the case of types of wood There are "choice cuttings" for lumber. This is a measure of the quality of work you've done and plan to do in the near future.

When you are looking at the log, it is necessary to look for circular lines or the rings on the ends, also known as annual rings. Each ring is the indicator of the new layer of wood that is added to trees every year. In certain kinds of wood, the rings are easily visible but they appear blurry in other. The wood close to the bark is known as sapwood is distinct from the inside heartwood.

Green wood is more supple in weight and more heavy than dry timber. the sapwood of green wood is much softer than the heart due to the sap or water that is contained within the wood. The more water a green log is able to hold the more it will shrink. The wood starts to dry out and shrink once the tree is removed. The sapwood that is soaked with water shrinks more rapidly and faster than the heart, as a result it is located on the outside and having a more barer. The log shrinks most within the line of annual rings.

Additionally, due to the uneven shrinking the log is more likely to split or break open, whereas near the edges cracks are running into the center. In the event that the piece is divided in half, or perhaps quartered and the interior areas are exposed, cracks aren't as severe because drying occurs more evenly throughout. Beams, joists planks or boards made from a log have the same tendency to shrink in a erratic manner, as the log that it was taken from. This results in them being irregular in shape and can be warped or curled (depending on the section of the tree from which they're taken). So, pieces taken from the middle of a log will retain its shape better than when it was cut from one end.

An aspiring woodworker has a lot to think about when selecting his wood. However, one crucial thing to bear in mind is making sure you choose straight-grained plain woodinstead of the soft and workable wood.

In addition to the fact that heartwood is usually superior to sapwood, it must be thought of that the wood of the young tree is stronger than the older one. Because it is closest to the heart that is why trees that are young tend to be the strongest strong, strongest, and most durable one, whereas the heartwood in an older tree is soft and not as strong as the one that is young.

One must consider the range of functions for the wood that will be utilized. The elasticity and the toughness of the wood need to be considered too. When we talk about elasticity, it doesn't mean that the wood bends and doesn't break. It also means that it does not bend breaking, but it is capable of returning to its original shape after being released. For toughness, on the other side, the wood should be flexible enough to bend without breaking, and not have to return to its original form when released. Also elastic wood should be tough to the point of breaking point, while the tough wood might have only a little elasticity. Both of these qualities can be found and are present in various levels in all kinds of wood.

The following is a listing of woods, but not the complete list. This list could be useful to novices:

Apple (fine-looking fine-grained, smooth, and slightly tough) It is utilized to turn, for example handles or handles. Also, for other smaller tasks.

Ash (flexible hard, durable, and elastic) It is employed for agricultural tools flooring, carriage-building, flooring as well as interior finishes, cabinet-work and more. It is generally coarse and has a straight-grained texture , and the majority of kinds are easy to work with.

Beech (close-grained wood that is solid, hard and strong and has a great polish) is extensively used in handles, machine-frames and plane-stocks, certain kinds of furniture, as well as many other minor items however, it is unlikely to be required by the beginner.

Birch (close-grained and a majority of kinds are strong and hard and are not difficult to use) It is utilized for flooring, furniture and interior finishes as well as turning and many other objects. Not just suitable for canoes, but it can be used to make skis, paddles, and other similar items.

Cherry (fine-grained and of moderate hardness, not hard to work on, and with gorgeous reddish-brown or yellowish-brown color) It is employed to finish interior and cabinet work as well as for a variety of other uses. For beginners, it is best to choose the straight and soft-grained varieties since some of the tougher and dense types are more difficult to smooth.

Cottonwood (soft light, supple and fine-grained) It is used for woodenware, boxes pulp, and many more.

Elm (strong strong, tough, and long-lasting, typically tough, flexible, and heavy) It is utilized in a few of its categories for frame construction of boats, agricultural equipment, yokes, wheel-hubs chairs, cooperage and many other uses.

Holly (quite hard, coarse-grained and white (but doesn't retain the pureness of its color) It is utilized for small items of cabinet-work and also for turning.

Lancewood (distinguished by its elasticity) It is utilized to make bows, fishing rods, and other such items.

Maple (close-grained and hard, sturdy heavy, and with an ethereal yellowish, reddish or brownish-white hue often almost white although it can be found in different shades) It is utilized extensively in cabinet work and flooring, interior finishing machines-frames, work-benches making, turning and for a vast assortment of different items. Beginners should stick beginning with the soft and straight-grained types, since the other types are difficult to work and smooth.

Oak (hard and robust flexible, strong and stiff (except for steaming, at which point it bends]and tough when exposed to weather or the soil) It is utilized to serve a myriad of functions that are too numerous to list including the construction of ships and buildings to agricultural equipment and furniture such as carriages, etc.

Pine (light and stiff, straight-grained and made of close fibre is easy to work, quickly nailed, and can be given an excellent finish) There isn't a better choice for beginners than white, clear pine for all purposes that it can be used for.

Spruce (light and straight-grained and generally free of knots) It is utilized for carpentry, interior finishes flooring, fencing and other woodwork that is not as good. Good quality Spruce is a good choice for paddles or spars, as well as other similar things and is a great choice for this type of work.

The Whitewood (brittle but soft however extremely light and easy to work widely used in wood) is utilized in the arts of working and is makes a great wood for beginning efforts of the novice.

There are a variety of ways to cut the wood correctly according to the project you are working on. How you cut the wood is important however you may believe that all important is cutting it into pieces.

When cut into boards or plansks, the center part of the log shrinks in size and thickness in the center, but it becomes thinner at the edges. It doesn't form a curl when cut into the center of the log, and it does not be curled in any way further.

The outside board shrinks the largest in width, and the least in thickness. Except the middle, each shrinks in a different way from the other, and then become convex towards the center, and then concave to the outside. Different types of wood shrink and warp in different amounts.

If you are looking for the beautifully drawn grain, that is typically observed in ash, oak, or chestnut, it can be achieved when cutting the log in the normal method. The annual rings which are cut diagonally, rather than the boards, or near the center, show the shape of the grain is going to be more prominent in the outside boards.

If you like the elegant image that appears when medullary rays appear on the surface on the table, then the log is made in the direction of the medullary rays (along these lines medullary Rays). This kind of sawing process requires greater effort and consumes more wood, which is why it costs more.

If you're looking for boards that be the thinnest in size and stay as similar as you can the log should be cut the log using radiatal lines to ensure that all boards will originate from the middle.

Always ensure that you get well-seasoned wood ready for use. If the wood is not completely dry prior to utilize it will probably result in cracks, open joints or warping and could even destroy your whole project. There are two methods of drying wood One is the traditional method (commonly called weather-drying or seasoning or air-drying) where the wood is slowly dried by naturally occurring exposure to air (but shielded from weather) or, leaving it to dry by its own. Another is the synthetic method (known as the process of kiln-drying). This is accomplished by keeping the wood in a space and drying it rapidly with steam or some other form of heating. This method can complete the job efficiently and quicker than the previous method.

It is said that it takes a while for timber to"season". It isn't true. The whole thing depends on the wood depending on its type shape and size, its atmospheric condition and other circumstances. Wood will never be perfect dry, regardless of whether it's dry enough to be suitable for your needs.

Chapter 8: Selecting The Best Wood to Use

To ensure that your project is durable and of the highest quality, you must select the correct kind of wood. Here are a few guidelines to aid you in choosing the appropriate kind of wood to complete your work:

You should think about the best options for the building you're planning to construct.

Do you need to use soft or hard wood? The answer is dependent on the type of furniture you're planning to build. If you're planning to build a luxurious dining table or queen-sized bed wood is a great option. If you're building a workbench , or simply a study table you could choose pine plywood.

Softwoods are evergreen trees whereas hardwoods are derived from flowers of trees. Although some softwoods are hard, hardwoods tend to be more durable and stable, so they are ideal for construction. Softwoods however can be used for carving.

Here are the most commonly used hardwoods:

Red Ash

White Ash

Beech

Yellow Birch

Balsa

European Ash from Europe

Cherry

Butternut

Kingwood

Rosewood

Sycamore

Purpleheart

Teak

Tulipwood

Lime

Mahogany

Walnut

Ebony

Maple

Kingwood

Oak

Here's a list of most commonly used softwoods:

Cedar

Fir

Larch

Pine

Redwood

Yew

If you're looking for durability you should consider using Chestnut, Iroko, Spanish Cedar and Oak wood.

Think about the cost.

If you're trying to stay within your budget it's a great option to choose pine wood. The wood is prone to cracks, however it's cheap and readily available. Beware of using expensive woods such as the ebony, sandalwood, purple heart, and Dalbergia however, as much as you can, you should choose the most expensive wood you can afford.

Be sure to look for these characteristics:

For a top-quality project, you must pick only the highest quality wood. When selecting the best wood for your woodworking project you should consider the following aspects:

Hardness - Be aware that there are many hardwoods that are not hard as well, and all softwoods may not be the same. Therefore, it is crucial to measure the strength of the wood, and not rely only upon its classification as a botanical. In general hardwoods are more durable and more valuable than softwood.

Grading – Not all hardwoods are created equal, therefore you must consider the quality of wood. If you're looking to construct furniture of high-quality then you must make use of FAS and FAS 1FACE Sound Wormy, Selects, and no. 1 Common.

Consider your skill level.

For those who are just beginning to learn you should use the pine and fir. They're not the same quality as mahogany or maple however they are more comfortable to handle. Therefore, you can work with pine at first, and then switch to better quality wood later after you've learned the art of woodworking.

Wood types

Here's a list of top woods you can work with to make woodworking tools:

Oak

This is one of the most commonly used hardwood. It's heavy, and has a light-colored. It is typically used for English and American designs in woodworking.

Image Source: wood-database.com

Maple

There are around 115 varieties of maple. Some are very hard while others are soft. Hard maple is so hard that it's difficult to use. If you're just starting out is best to use soft maple.

Cedar

It is a reddish-colored wood that is quite soft. It is straight and it has a wonderful smell. It is perfect for outdoor furniture like patio tables as it is able to withstand humid areas.

Fir

It has a distinct straight, smooth and reddish brown hue. It is typically employed for construction, but because it's comparatively inexpensive the wood is frequently employed for furniture production, too.

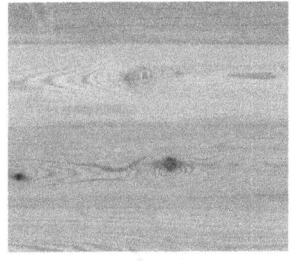

Pine

Photograph Source: realsimple.com

This is the ideal option for novices since it's cheap and easy to use. It's also great to carve. But, it's best not to making use of this technique if you're creating an elegant piece of furniture, such as the wooden table, sofa or a bed with intricate details.

Redwood

It is commonly employed for outdoor furniture due to it is extremely resistant to water. It is straight and has reddish hue. It's not inexpensive but it's not costly neither.

Ash

Ash is straight and, just like pine it is a breeze to use.

Birch

There are two kinds of birch trees: as well as yellow. It is easily available and definitely less expensive than other hardwoods. It is durable and is extremely easy to work with.

Cherry

It is easy to locate cherry wood. It's a dark reddish brown color , and is often used in furniture making and woodworking. It is a breeze to work with however it's a bit more expensive than oak or maple.

Mahogany

This is among the most beautiful furniture woods. It has a brownish red hue and is extremely sturdy. It's able to withstand stain and you'll only have to apply a single coating of varnish for a glossy appearance.

Poplar

It is among the hardwoods that are less expensive. It is very soft and comfortable to use. It is an excellent option for drawers. It's sturdy.

Teak

It is a very rare kind of wood, but it is the perfect choice for furniture that can be used outdoors. It's weatherproof and is stunning and beautiful, too. It has a golden-brown hue and an oily feeling.

Walnut

It is a breeze to use and is great for big projects like queen-size beds and dining tables. It is also expensive.

Keep in mind that when it comes to woodworking, it's the grade of wood that matters paramount. However, if you're just an aspiring woodworker, you should try to select the types of wood that are simpler to use. When you get more advanced into the next stage, you could use more durable as well as more costly wood.

Chapter 9: Woodworking Tips And Techniques

Woodworking can be a challenge for those who are just beginning their journey into this field. But, you'll develop new techniques as you progress. This chapter will cover the various techniques and tips you must learn about woodworking.

Security Rules in Woodworking

Before beginning woodworking, it's important that you are aware of the safety guidelines since you'll be using a lot of powerful and sharp tools. The rules for woodworking come from common sense however, not following the guidelines can lead to injuries. Here are the safety rules that you must follow in case you are planning to pursue woodworking as a pastime.

Wear protective equipment

It is essential to use the proper personal safety equipment that includes hearing protection as well as latex gloves, masks as well as safety eyewear. When you work with wood you'll have to be able to handle a lot of noise, dust, and splinters. Do not begin task without making sure you are wearing the. Additionally, it is essential to dress in comfortable clothes that protect your body from the impact of falling wood chip.

Avoid drinking alcohol prior to working

Drinking intoxicants and woodworking isn't a good combination. Although it might seem safe to sip a glass of beer prior to working on an undertaking, alcohol could make your senses be numb, no matter the amount you've consumed. It can impair your judgment which can be dangerous since it puts yourself at risk of injuring yourself.

Always disconnect the Power before changing the Blades

If you are in the need to switch tools, ensure that you remove the device from the electrical outlet to ensure the motor is actually shut off. Many woodworkers have lost fingers due to not following this principle.

Make use of an Extension Cord

When you are working with drill bits or any electrical equipment that has to be moved around, make use of an extension cord to ensure that you are able to move throughout the workspace without the necessity of plugging and unplug power.

Make sure to use sharp blades and bits.

A dull cutter can be dangerous to use and will make it difficult to complete a task when you are using dull blades. Therefore, prior to starting work ensure that all the blades you use are sharp.

Do not be distracted by any distractions

Distractions can be found everywhere. However, when you're using sharp instruments it is recommended to stay clear of them so that you do not lose concentration.

Joinery Techniques

A skilled woodworker can to create seamless joinery. Joinery is the act of joining two pieces to make the final end product. It usually refers to joining joints made by woodworking. This article will talk about joining techniques you can employ for woodworking projects.

Joints can make or break a project. It is crucial to note that the more challenging the joint you select the more durable the final product will be. Here are some types of joints woodworkers may make use of to complete their various projects.

Illustration of Types of Joints

Butt joint is an easy way to join two pieces of wood around the corner or at both sides. But, this kind of joint isn't durable, but it can be reinforced with screws, glue or nails.

Dado joint Dado joint frequently used for joining shelves for books. The dado joint is defined as making a cut in one piece of wood, which is then receptacled to the opposite end.

Dowel joint joint is made by drilling holes that align every piece of wood. The two pieces are put together to form a strong joint. This is a tricky process since it requires a tool for centering to make sure everything is in alignment.

Lap joint Lap joints are like the butt joint, but a rabbet can be cut in one piece of wood to ensure both pieces overlap. To keep the wood with a screw glue and nail can be used to tighten the joints.

Miter joints are created by cutting both ends the wood which will be joined at an angle that is 45°. It requires accurate cutting and measuring of the angle to make an even and straight end product.

Mortise and Tenon Joint The mortise and tenon joint a classic joints that was utilized by woodworkers from time immemorial. It is a sturdy joint that can be made more durable by the addition of an additional peg.

Through dovetail joint joints are valued for their design and durability. It requires patience and precision to cut the joints that interlock. The joint gives a distinctive visual look for the construction.

The tongue-and-groove joint kind of joint permits the shrinkage of wood. It is usually used for wood that shrinks in time. To create this joint, you need to cut an edging at the edge from one wood piece. On the other piece of wood create an appropriate tongue to fit into the groove.

A biscuit joining device which cuts slots of oval shape in the workpieces mating to allow them to be securely glued.

Clamping Techniques

Clamping permits you to make the glue set as it is drying. It also keeps the whole structure from moving as the glue is set. Here are some clamping techniques can be used to hold the glue once it sets.

Technique Description Illustration

Secure odd-shaped shapes using heavy bags . You can create your own way of clamping your woodwork using the weight of a lead bag or sand. This can help you save dollars when purchasing expensive clamps that be used to hold wood pieces with odd shapes.

Utilize long bar clamps for clamping carcasses When clamping a carcass the most efficient way to accomplish this is to use long clamps that allow the carcase to be suspended.

Tapered blocks can be used to clamp sides that are sloped. You can create tapered blocks using 3/8 " block of wood scraps.

Make sure that the block is 2" bigger and 1" larger than the length of the item being clamped. It is possible to use tapered blocks to secure items with sloping surfaces.

Utilize felt pads to guard the woodwork's surface. clamping may cause scratches and nicks to the woodwork's surface. To safeguard the woodwork ensure that you apply the felt pad (self-adhesive ones) onto the clamps in order they act as protection pads for furniture.

Make use of a clothespin to secure tiny details when gluing pieces of stock or wood using a standard clamp may be difficult due to the fact that they put too much pressure and could crack the woodwork. Instead, try using clothespins to hold small details.

Methods for measuring and marking

Woodworking requires you to be capable of taking accurate measurements and markings on wood. The achievement of any project depends on the precision with which you take the required measurements. Here are the marking and measuring guidelines that you should be aware of in woodworking.

If you plan to measure less than one inches, it's crucial to use a sturdy metal ruler. The tape measure is flexible, so the measurement you take could not be precise.

Use one tape measurement for the building process of your project. The issue with using different tape measurements is that there may be a difference in the measurement's graduations.

If you cut the lumber to length ensure you place one end in a square before you mark the line. This will ensure you do not make any mistakes when measuring the length.

The end that is riveted of the tape measure could result in inaccurate measurements as time passes. Therefore, avoid using the riveted part and align one" measurement with the square edge of your workpiece.

Make use of a mechanical pencil for any marking work as it produces a narrow, fine line that doesn't leave any doubt about the area you must cut. You may also make use of a lead pencil, however, make sure it's sharp.

Utilize an x-square use a square to trace your wooden pieces to the length. You can make an erect line that is perpendicular with the edge of the blade.

Finishing Tips and Methods

The correct finish you apply to your wood pieces could affect the final product. Therefore, it is essential to be armed with useful information on how to make the most effective finish for the woodwork projects you are working on.

Surface coatings: They offer a clear finishes. They also offer added protection for the wood. Examples of coatings for the surface include varnish, lacquer and even shellac.

Finishes with pigments: These finishing are not transparent and appear like paint. Examples of colored finishes are black lacquer. They are also available in natural finishes and are akin to the natural hue of wood.

Penetrating finish: As the name suggests, these finishes go through the grain of wood instead of being set on the surface. This gives it an extremely natural appearance. They also provide less luster to wood.

However here are some techniques that you can apply to apply the finishing touches to your workpieces.

Waxing: Waxing is fantastic technique can be used to add finishing to your wood. It's laborious, however it offers additional protection to your wood. Also, waxing is utilized to renew older finishes on wood. While labor-intensive the process isn't requiring any maintenance. Waxing can be applied on the surface of the finish to penetrate it.

Staining: Staining can be used to enhance the natural color in the wood. It creates uniformity within the wood. This is particularly beneficial if the wood is inconsistent in appearance.

Toning or glazing Toning and toning are two ways that are used to add some highlights for the wood and enhance the color that the timber has. Both of these techniques can be employed to give an aged appearance to the wood.

The two types of finishing are liming or picking. Both picking and liming are two kinds of traditional finishes that can be used to highlight the natural grain in the wood. This is accomplished through the use of two distinct (contrasting) hues that comprise the base color, and a different color which is rubbed into the grain.

Bleaching is employed to reduce the color of wood or eliminate any discoloration caused by moisture. But, it is crucial to keep in mind that this technique isn't able to remove stains or dyes.

Distressing is used to create an the appearance of aging and texture the wood. This can be accomplished by sanding the finish once it has dried, or by rubbing a solvent to wash away the paint.

Chapter 10: Different Kinds Of Wood

Hardwood Vs Softwood

The two main categories which woods can be divided into are softwood and hardwood Be careful, but don't take a chance with the names. Hardwood is not always a hard material and softwood isn't always soft. The trees that have leaves and flowers typically are hardwood while coniferous (with needles) evergreens are softwoods. The price of hardwood is greater than softwoods, probably because of its accessibility. The investment in hardwood is worthwhile for those who require a solid piece of furniture such as tables, beds, and so on. If you are looking for a unique or carved wooden item to improve the appearance of your living space You can choose the softwood with no doubt.

Wood types

I am thrilled to share with you the most well-known kinds of wood that are used in the construction of furniture. I'm hoping you'll be able to make the wise choice after reading this. Also, I am sure you'll be able to appreciate the value of wood as well as the amount of beauty it adds to our interior. Beginning with the types of hardwood Let's explore the options.

Hardwoods

Oak

Oak is among the most popular woods used to make furniture. It is also known for its over 60 varieties of oak that are grown in the US. It is classified into two kinds: Red as well as black, as well as white oak. White oak is a grayish brown hue while red oak has the reddish hue. White oak is believed to be more expensive contrasted to the red.

Properties

It is used in furniture made of solid wood because of its durability and gorgeous grain. The rough texture and noticeable grain is due to nature of the large conductive vessels that are laid out in the summer months instead of later. There are medullar streaks or medullar medullar medullar in quarter-sawed lumber of oak.

Uses

It is commonly used to create English as well as American design patterns for the country. It is well-known for its reproduction of Gothic or William and Mary or numerous pieces that transition from one to the next.

Cherry

It is thought of as an expensive wood , and is found in the eastern part in the US. It is extremely valuable and it is not possible to employ hand tools for it. It is also known as fruitwood. You might like vintage furniture made from cherry that look brand fresh even after many years. It could change to a more rich brown or red with time.

Properties

The cherry's color ranges in light reddish to deep brown. It can be enhanced by adding a stain it. It is a great material to make furniture and cabinets. The closed grain feature makes it simple to polish and doesn't require fillers. It is possible to be creative by mixing cherry furniture with any other wood since it has the capability of matching any other woodwork you have in your house.

Uses

It is a well-known material used in the construction of furniture in the 18th century. The solids and veneers made of cherry are often used in those who prefer

French or Colonial designs. The various applications make it very flexible.

Mahogany

There are a variety of kinds and varieties of mahogany based on the region in which it is being produced. Honduras Mahogany is native and is found in Africa, South America and Central America. The price varies based on its quality Mahogany. It is believed that African logs are believed to be lower quality and a log from the Caribbean is renowned for its high-quality, hardness and durability. Philippians mahogany is easily bought at a low cost since it's not attractive and durable, even though the color is similar.

Properties

The mahogany color ranges between medium and deep brown. It has a distinct grain with a uniform pores. It shows stripse, ripple and ribbon-like look. It has a nice finish and is thought to be an excellent carving wood.

Uses

It is extensively utilized extensively in Victorian style furniture as well as in the design of modern furniture.

Maple

The maple tree has 115 species, of which just 5 species are found in the US and commercially grown. It's impervious to moisture, making it more much more durable than other types of wood.

Properties

It is the strongest wood and it is costly because of its durability. It is also used for floors in bowling alleys since it's immune to the effects of shocks. It also has pores that are fine, creating a smooth texture and grain. The grain can be curly, wavy and leaves-like characters. It's light brown in the color and can withstand staining and paint.

Uses

It is used to create an instrument's back, and love its designs. The maple is utilized for butcher blocks, and is strong enough to handle power tools alone. Bedroom furniture made of Maple that you intend to maintain for a long period of time would be a better choice. The early 90's American Colonial furniture was built out of Maple extensively, and is now thought of as antique.

Walnut

It is one of the well-known and adaptable of woods and can be located throughout Asia, America and Europe. If you want to purchase furniture of the highest quality it is best to be looking for walnut wood. It was utilized in the past, but it is still popular. Its color ranges from light-colored to dark brown with streaks of purple. European and American walnut have distinctive characteristic.

Properties

Furniture made from walnut wood is lightweight however it is extremely durable and sturdy. It has a beautiful grain and can take finishes extremely well. It is used to make cabinets. European walnut is believed as"the "King of Kings". It's light in appearance when compared the American black walnut, and also is smooth and fine. Its broad range of applications makes it one of the most sought-after and well-worth a look. Characteristics such as stripes, crotches curly curls, burls, curls and mottles.

Uses

Walnut was used for cabinet making, particularly in the 18th century.

Teak

It is an additional expensive wood that is available in a shades of golden yellow to dark brown, with dark and light streaks. It is typically found throughout Southeast Asia but is grown in Africa as well.

Properties and uses

It can be used to create solid or veneer pieces. It's sturdy, heavy, and long-lasting. It's distinctive and has a straight grain. It can be used for flooring or doors. Natural oil is emitted from teak, which makes it be able to withstand different weather conditions and resist cracks and decay. Oriental furnishings were constructed from teak.

Rosewood

The beautiful wood is famous for its high-quality scent, its fragrant nature and its the ability to be close-grained. You'll be impressed by its color that can range from dark brown to deep purple, with noticeable black streaks. It's a valuable material and looks stunning when used in the manufacture of musical instruments such as furniture, piano casings or veneers as well as art projects. It is difficult to form using hand tools.

Sycamore

Its ability to resist splitting makes it a favorite among the butcher block. Its reddish-pinkish color and low cost make it an excellent choice for those who do not require costly furniture. Hand tools are ideal for Sycamore.

Basswood

Another common, inexpensive wood is Basswood. It is straight and even grain. It's pleasant to look at when paired with other rare woods such as Mahogany or Walnut. It is a beautiful color that ranges from creamy white to a creamy brown. It has tiny pores and is very fine.

Ash

Ash is another reasonably priced wood used to create furniture that will require some bent. There are sixteen species that are produced across the east of the United States but white ash is the most commonly used. It is a kind of hardwood that is used for bent furniture components structural frames and also provides added strength.

It is a the appearance of a creamy white color or gray with a slight brown hue. Ash's grain is similar to the grain of oak.

Beech

It's also a low-cost wood that is pale in color and is well-known for its ability to bend. It is found in the eastern portion in the United States. While it's not utilized as much as the Ash (most likely because it's not very eye-catching) however, it is possible to make furniture pieces that aren't at the forefront of attention or are placed in secluded locations. Like drawer bottoms or sides or backs of cabinets.

It's great with staining, and is stained as mahogany, cherry , or maple. It is not recommended for hand tools due to its toughness.

Hickory

There are fifteen species of hickory trees that are grown in the eastern part of the United States.8 Some of these are significant and are used for commercial use.

The moderately priced, hard and sturdy Hickory is the ideal option for lawn furniture including chairs, rockers and Windsor veneers. It has a brown to reddish brown hue and is extremely heavy. Hand tools aren't suitable for working with. It's a closed grain and does not come with numerous figures.

Elm

Elm is expensive due to its superb bend properties. It is not often found since its trees have been destroyed due to Dutch Elm disease. It's lighter medium brown or dark brown and has streaks of red. It's suitable for furniture at home and in offices. Restaurant owners should not be afraid to make use of it as furniture even though it's intended to be used outdoors.

Birch

Birch can be found in the northeast US in the northeast US and Canada. People are enthralled by the light brown wood with a yellowish tint because of its beautiful grain pattern. It is hard and heavy utilized for a wide variety of doors and furniture. It can also be used for cabinets and floors. Its only downside is the cost. It is a moderately costly hardwood.

Softwoods

Pine

More than 100 species pine can be found across the globe. It is cultivated in the Northern northern hemisphere.

Properties

Its color is light yellow and light, making it simple to move. It is soft wood that does not shrink or expand. It has no figure and is straight-grained.

Uses

Pine with knots is utilized to make decorative pieces of wood. It is also used in country and provincial furniture. While it's not very long-lasting, the price is affordable and it is widely used by people of all ages. It requires a primer for an even finish. The it should be applied prior to staining. It is possible to create a wooden box for jewelry and other important items.

Cedar

The beautiful and durable wood is perfect for creating cabinets as well as the lining for cabinets. It is fragrant and is able to deter moths.

It is a highly regarded lightweight wood with a fine grain. Cedar is resistant to extreme climate changes. Beware of bleaching or staining cedar.

Redwood

The most amazing thing about redwood is that the age of its trees is at least 2,500 years, and they can grow up to 300 feet in height. The trees are found in the Pacific United States, it is thought to be the most suitable for outdoor furniture because of its resistance to elements of the weather like moisture sun, bugs and moisture. It is deep in reddish brown color , and growth rings. It is possible to manage redwood using hand tools, and the price varies from region to region.

Spruce

It is a softwood that is strong but not heavy in weight. It is used to create boxes as ladders, crates and for general millworks. It is able to shrink and offers lower resistance to the wear and tear.

Fir

It is suitable to make a range of furniture making projects such as windows, doors, doors, plywood frames, veneer, frames and millwork. Golden and brown colors can be enhanced with stain. This wood is not an extremely strong resistance to decay.

Hemlock

Hemlock has a consistent texture and is extremely lightweight in weight. Its capacity to take glue and screw grippers allows it to be used on any type of furniture. It can also be used to construct things like panels and sub flooring. It can also be used to make crates, doors, planks, and boards. Hand tools as well as power tools are simple to work with this kind of wood. The strength and durability of this wood and its durability towards wear and tear make it a popular material for cabinets windows, ladders, and window frames. Western variety of Hemlock is preferred opposed to the eastern variety because of its resin-free quality. It has a smooth finish and is able to take any stain.

I'm hoping that the information above will help you to pick the best wood for your furniture , and even to identify the exact type of wood being used to make the piece you're planning to purchase. Alder chestnut, apple, cottonwood, cypress magnolia, pearwood, hackberry willow, mesquite, and numerous other types of wood are used to serve a variety of purposes. Each kind is recognized for its unique properties and every piece of furniture provides clues as to what kind of wood is utilized in its design. The more you learn about it and learn about it, the more you'll understand.

Chapter 11: What to Maintain Woodworking Tools

In order to become a skilled woodworker You must learn how to care for tools. Regular maintenance will make sure that your tools will be more effective and require less physical effort to complete a task. This will also extend the life span of your equipment and reduce the cost.

By ensuring regular maintenance, you'll improve the durability of your tools. If a saw is well kept, then you'll be able to be sure that it can be able to cut through wood without using excessive wood or using the use of too much physical effort.

Here's how to effectively maintain your workshop tools:

Proper storage

It is essential to make sure that every tool is in its appropriate place inside the workshop, the toolbox, or workshop. Do not store tools in a haphazard manner.

Lubricate moving parts

Every moving part must be greased as often as is. If you have the electric drill make sure that the parts moving oil- or grease-filled according to the instructions of the manufacturer. Even if your power tool is functioning properly, it is important to ensure it's oiled according to schedule.

Avoid exposing metallic parts to water.

Be sure that all the metallic parts of your woodwork tools aren't exposed water. That means that you need to ensure that your tools are kept in a dry area. This will stop rusting and will prolong the life for the instrument.

Make use of the right tools for the task.

If you're looking to bend wood, but don't have access to the chisel you need, would you be using a big screwdriver that is flat? Do you have the claw hammer instead mallets? If the answer is "yes then you're wrong. Never make use of the wrong tool to accomplish an objective. When you use a screwdriver, you'll cause it to weaken and, consequently, reduce its life span.

Service electric gadgets

It is also important to make sure that all appliances are maintained whenever possible or as suggested by the manufacturer.

What to Go About Woodworking

For those who are new to woodworking, it may appear like a difficult and challenging job. But, after you've built your first piece of wood and you'll see that woodworking is a breeze. Here's a step-by procedure on how to construct the woodworking product.

Step 1: Contemplate.

Before you construct any piece it is essential to know what you're planning to construct. Are you planning to build an armchair, table or wall unit? What type of table or chair are you planning to build? What size will the table or chair be? What is the best place to put the thing you plan to construct? Do you intend to build it for personal use , or for commercial use? If it's for commercial use Do you have an existing market? If you've got a market or the product is already pre-ordered, you'll likely be limited in time to complete the task.

When you have a clear understanding of all of the above questions You'll be able to figure out the requirements to start. When you're creating something to private use you'll have the time you require. You'll be able to modify or make any adjustments you'd like when building an item intended for use by a person for their own personal needs.

Step 2 Step 2: Visualize.

If you've got an idea of the product you wish to create, you need to determine what you would like it to appear. This involves determining particulars of the item you're planning to construct. If you are planning to build an chopping board, which shape do you want? Are you looking for circular or rectangular board? If you're planning to create the table, what would the top appear? What number of legs will the table be built on?

Step 3: Make an outline or sketch that shows the product.

The third step is to create the layout or drawing of the object you wish to construct. This step is vital because it allows you visualize elements that you'd thought of when you were visualizing. If you'd not thought of the supporting structures of your chair, it will be easier to be able to recall the elements after drawing them. In this point, you'll be able to seek out other opinions and their opinions on the design you'd like to design. You may also make changes to the sketch.

In order to get an accurate picture of the object you're planning to construct You can make multiple drawings, each one depicting the object from a different perspective. The drawing can be used to determine the exact dimensions of the object you'd like to construct. If you're making tables, you could make a rectangular one with a top measures 3 feet by 4 feet. When you have the precise dimensions of the object you're planning to construct it is easy to determine the required components.

Step 4: list different parts

The fourth step is to create a list of all the elements of the object you're planning to construct. Also, you must record the dimensions of each one of the parts listed. You could, for instance, decide to build chairs that consist of the top portion (measuring the dimensions of 3 feet x 4 feet x one inches) as well as 4 legs (each one measuring 2.5 inches by 2.5 inches in size by three feet). Medium high density fibreboard (MDF) can also be utilized as the top in the table.

Step 5: List raw materials.

After you've made an outline of the various components of the product you wish to construct, you will be able to easily create an inventory of the required raw materials. Therefore, you should make an inventory of the raw materials you'll require. You must ensure that you have included the amount of each component needed. An example of raw materials include vanish, nails, filler material and a bit of medium dense fiber board.

Step 6: Purchase raw materials

If you are aware of the things you require to begin You can now buy the materials needed to begin. Be very cautious when buying raw materials to ensure that your project is successful. For instance, it is recommended to purchase more durable steel nails if you intend to utilize hardwood. After being hammered, soft nails might break instead of piercing the hardwood. If you're planning on building something that is going to be put in the bathroom or kitchen it is recommended to use hardwood rather than softwood. This is due to the fact that hardwoods are more durable than softwoods when put in watery areas.

Step 7: Create a plan for the project.

Now you must plan the method you'll use to carry out the plan. It is important to consider the way you'll begin and how you'll take the next step. What part of the table will you start with? For instance, you could decide to begin with the four legs prior to making the top portion of the table. Also, you must plan out the time you'll finish the project. If you can, create an agenda (work program) and put in the effort to meeting the objectives you set out.

Step 8: Ensure you have all the equipment.

This involves looking through the workshop or toolbox as to ensure you have everything you'll require. If you plan to build an chopping board it is essential that you have the saw, emery papers and tape measurement.

Step 9: Start building different parts.

Now you can begin building every one of the various parts of the object you wish to construct. In the case of the table, you can construct the legs first, then the top piece. You may decide to begin with the smaller , more difficult to carve pieces before building the larger and easier to build pieces.

Step 10 Step 10: Make sure you assemble (join) the various parts.

After you've built all the components, you are able to proceed to put them together into one unit. Also, you should employ this filler to cover in all the dents that are present in the final product. Put the product in a dry and cool place for a period of time (a couple of hours) to let the filler substance dry.

Step 11: Complete.

It is now time to do the final touches. This involves sandpapering the piece and then removing any filler material. It is also important to make sure that the item is structurally solid and will be used for the purpose it was designed to serve. If you're creating an armchair, you should be sure it's able to comfortably stand up to an average adult who sits on it. To test the strength of its construction make sure you hold it tightly and then try shaking it vigorously. You may also be able to place it on your back while carrying more weight in order to simulate the situation in which someone with a lot of weight will be perched on the surface. If it is still intact it is likely that it's strong enough to meet its needs.

Step 12 Step 12: Painting.

The final step involves lacquering, painting, or varnishing of the product. This is a crucial step because it determines the quality of the final product. A beautiful item is likely to fetch more attention if you decide to market it. If you're making it to use for your own personal enjoyment it is possible to apply paint or varnish which matches the overall design of your home.

Chapter 12: Choosing the Right Tools for The Job

The first time you begin working with wood, you'll be wondering whether you've got the tools needed for the task. The issue with starting with a new pastime like this is that you will require a variety of tools for many different tasks.

If you've never completed some woodwork before it's possible that you'll be a bit overwhelmed. To help you, I've provided the tools you're likely to require. Be aware that you may not have all these tools at first However, as you grow more proficient and comfortable, you'll require more.

Tape measures

Whatever type or wood that you're dealing on or the basic layout you're working on will require tape measures. I suggest using the retractable tape measure because they're much more convenient to use than non-retractable models. Find an instrument that is equipped with an locking device and a hook on the bottom to the measure. These features will allow you get precise measurements in just a few minutes.

Hammer with claw

The claw hammer can be an essential tool, in my opinion. There are many different sizes of claw hammers on the market however I would recommend getting one that's not overly heavy.

Utility knife

Any utility knife that comes with an simple locking mechanism can be very beneficial. Make sure you find one with disposable blades that you can replace. It is likely that even the simplest and cheapest of utility knives can be especially useful when it comes to making marks on wood or cutting out tiny paper templates.

6 inch square layout

If there were a tool that could be described as "The Most Useful" in the world of woodworking most likely it's The layout square. It makes marking out an outline so simple and is also the best when you need to measure the 45-degree angle. It's relatively inexpensive, and this efficient tool will to ensure that you are taking the right measurements.

Level

It's vitally important that, when you design something you can be sure it's either horizontal or vertical. Levels are the best tool to utilize, and are extremely useful. Even skilled woodworkers, who know whether something is level must utilize this tool because the work needs to be precise to a tiniest degree.

If you begin with a small amount and progress to larger jobs it is possible that you will find the transition from a short level to a long-term level as you require it beneficial.

Chisels

No matter what kind of task you're planning to complete, you'll require the chisel. You should purchase one that's sharpened and then utilize it to get rid of the waste. Don't think that one chisel can be used for all tasks, you'll require several in line with the project you're creating. Make sure you purchase a good quality set of chisels which have a variety of sizes.

Sliding bevel

If you have for a duplicate angle you'll discover that sliding bevels come in extremely useful. A sliding bevel functions much like a layout square but it lets you adjust and then lock a portion of it, so that you can duplicate the angle once more.

Screwdrivers

Screwdrivers are another essential item, and I don't really need to elaborate on the reason. It is recommended to purchase more than one dimension and kind of screwdriver since you'll need various kinds (Flatheads and square heads, etc.) for various projects.

Block plane

A block plane will allow you cut away thin pieces of wood so you can polish it and use it to work with. This can also come in handy for cleaning the edges of a few edges, too.

What is the matter with power tools?

It is necessary to utilize power tools for the majority of woodworking projects since they make life significantly simpler. Power tools need not cost a lot If you're worried about being unable to pay for these tools, consider reconsidering your options.

Even the simplest power tools can be extremely effective, and you'll be able to use these tools for a lot of tasks, even though you're not an expert. The tools listed below are placed in order of priority starting with the most important tool higher in importance than the next one. This is the equipment you'll need to complete a variety of woodworking jobs completed.

Circular saw

Although it's often used in carpentry The circular saw is a versatile tool which you will find extremely useful. It makes cutting plywood and fiberboard an easy task and should be the first power tool you think of purchasing.

Power drill

The power drill can be a strong as well as a versatile device. But, don't purchase the first one you see since you'll have to choose which one is a keyless chuck an encased one such as a hammer or straight drill. If you're wondering I'm not recommending using the cordless drill because they can be expensive and do not perform as well. Opt for a electric drill, and you'll be glad you did.

Jigsaw

A jigsaw is a tool that allows you to cut circular or curved designs in wood. Also known as a 'Sabre saw the tool is great for beginner woodworker. Make sure you purchase a tool which allows you to switch the blade quickly.

Random orbital sander

With a variety of functions this sander is a fantastic power tool for everyone regardless of how knowledgeable you may be. This kind of sander could cost more than sandpaper, and palm sanders. However, the random movements are employed will lessen the number of sanding marks that are left on your work. Be sure to search for an sander that comes with discs to sand that are easy to locate.

Table saw

A table saw could be one of the most effective tools you'll ever purchase. Although it's not necessarily the first tool to consider buying, it's sure to end up being one of the best purchases you can make. Get the top table saw that you can afford, and you'll be glad you spent the money.

Compound miter saw

As you get more experienced, you'll soon be required to cut compound angles. This is where a mitersaw will make your life much simpler. The benefit is that once you've been able to cut with precision using miter saws, you will not require a circular saw nearly as often since the compound saw will be able to finish the work efficiently.

Router

A high-quality router is the most important power tool that I would recommend novices purchase. A fixed base router is the ideal tool for anyone who is just beginning working with wood since it can help you get the job accomplished with ease. I suggest using a router with a variable speed, not less than two HP and an easy-to-use bit-change feature. If you can access all of the above-mentioned power and hand tools, doing a range of projects becomes much more simple. Furthermore, as you gain experience you'll be able to use the tools you've chosen is a matter of routine.

Chapter 13: Modern Woodworking Tools Of Today

The latest Woodworking Tools are generally utilized by people who have more experience in the art. This is due to the fact that most of them are "power tools" that is, they require another source of power to operate. These tools are usually electrical, and the user needs to be aware of the proper and safe use. Incorrect use of these tools can cause injury or even death.

The power tool is one however, they are designed for beginners and are the ones which are suggested for those who is looking to woodwork in a modern manner.

This is the Random Orbit Sander

Random Orbit Sanders are electrical hand-held power tools that are used in woodworking, to smooth rough wood surfaces. This Random Orbit Sander has a

Sandpaper disk pad that executes two distinct actions, it spins the pad, and the gyrations of the entire pad assembly. The two actions when coupled with the motion of the hand of the user create an unique and random sanding pattern that leaves no swirl or marks. This Random Orbit Sander is the most popular tool to make a perfect and smooth wood surface.

The Router

The Router is considered to be the most flexible tool for woodworking that has been developed to date. It is used to make patterns, edging , and groove cuts. The Router is composed of an electric motor that is vertically mounted on a solid base housing. The electrical motor comes with an attached collet at the bottom of its shaft to which it is connected to a cutting piece. The cutting tool is able to be altered based on the kind of cut to be done. The height can be adjusted to allow for the cutting piece to protrude from the sole of the base housing. This can be done by altering the height of the motor mounting. This feature lets the woodworker to adjust the cutting depth of the wood surface. There are D-handles opposite sides of Router for controlling.

Router Bit Set

The Router cannot be complete without a collection of Router bits. They are Router bits are those that create the precise cut required for any type of routing. There are two kinds of Router bits: the straight ones and round-over pieces. Round-over bits feature bearings at the end that rotate in a free manner. They can be used to route around the edges of a piece of work when trimming. Woodworkers prefer round-over bits to trim because they don't require any type of fence for guide because the bearing takes care of this for them. Straight bits will not feature the tiny bearing at the other end since they are designed to pass through the middle of a board in order to create grooves. They are mostly used to cut grooves across the top of the boards.

Circular Saw

The Circular saw is essentially an electric motor with teethed blades or discs that rotates to cut through materials like wood, plastic and occasionally even metal. The blade of a circular saw can be changed depending on the material you wish to cut. In woodworking, it's utilized mostly in cutting sheets of wood as well as hardwood (if there is a broad enough surface to work on) and plywood MDF and many other.

Jigsaw

The function of a Jigsaw is to cut curving shapes. It is the reason it has the narrow blade which can be moved up and down. The blades cut along the upstroke , and that's why they are designed so that the teeth face up. There are a variety of blades into the jigsaw, based on the material you're cutting. It features a bevel sole plate on the bottom that serves as a guide for cutting curves in the wood.

Nail Gun

Nail guns can be used as modern methods to drive nails into various kinds of surfaces. In woodworking, they are employed to join the two wood pieces. Nail guns are typically driven with compressed air or gases like propane or butane. The nail gun has taken over the hammer as a most popular tool used for woodworking and carpentry.

Power Drill

Power drills are among of the most beneficial tools available. By changing a bit, you are able to drill holes as well as drive screws and many more. The motor drill functions as a hand-held motor that has the "chuck". The jaws on the tip of the drill hold it in place when you move the chuck to loosen or tighten it. A drill that has keyless chuck tightens or releases by simply twisting it by using your hands. This makes changing bits easy and quick. Key chucks require an instrument to hold the bit to secure it. It keeps the bit securely in place using greater force, so this kind of drill is generally employed on jobs with greater demands. To switch the bit, turn the collar to make jaws wide enough to allow the bit to slide into the hole, then twist it against the reverse direction, tightening the collar until it stops, and clicks.

Its trigger is the primary control. Variable speed drilling allows you to begin drilling slowly and then speed up according to the pressure that you place on the trigger, similar to driving the accelerator in your automobile. A button on the handle can alter the direction in which that you drill. Forward pulls the fastener into with a counterclockwise spin. You can set it to reverse to reverse the screws or back out the piece when it gets stuck. There is also an neutral position that secures the trigger. This helps prevent accidents when you're not drilling with the drill.

The type of drill you choose depends on the task at hand. Cordless drills run on rechargeable batteries, which are useful in situations where you aren't close to a power source. Cordless drills are an excellent choice for drilling into wood surfaces that are hard. It is possible to have both of them in your toolbox. Volts and amps show the power of the drill. When a drill is cordless, this is measured in voltage, while for the drill with a cord, it is expressed in amps. A higher number generally indicates heavier duty and more difficult to handle. Chucks are also available in various sizes. A smaller quarter-inch or 3/8 inch chuck is sufficient for tasks that require light effort. They are usually lighter and smaller, which is ideal for binding pieces of wood on walls so that your arms will not get tired. The larger half-inch chuck can handle bigger pieces, which is your ideal tool for jobs that require heavy-duty, such as drilling into hard surfaces. They are also larger and heavier.

Band Saw

The band saw is one of the most important tools for the woodworking shop. It can be used for various curving and straight cut. The band saw is able to handle many different sizes of stock, and does what other saws can do but then some. The blade of the band saw is a continuous piece of steel with teeth that runs through two wheels. The top wheel exerts tension, while the lower wheel supplies power to the motor via a set of pulleys. When the wheels rotate they rotate the blade downwards and create the cutting action in the saw. The downward movement also presses the material against the table which allows for perfect and precise cuts. There are guide blocks to stop the blade from sliding both ways. One of its strengths is its ability to cut curves with precision.

Scroll Saw

Scroll saws are fantastic tools for the woodshop. One of the best features of these saws is the fact that they're quiet and don't produce lots of dust. There are many options you can make with a scrollsaw, including delicate ornaments you could present as gifts and intarsias (a woodworking process that involves different sizes and shapes of wood that are arranged to create a mosaic that gives the impression of depth) as well as many other. Scroll saws feature extremely fine blades that let you reach those places that a regular band saw cannot. They're extremely safe to use and are the perfect option to help kids get started with woodworking.

Table Saw

Table Saws Table Saw is basically a circular saw blade that extends from the table's surface. The table functions as a base for any material needs to be passed through the saw to cut. Table saws are an essential tool particularly if you work on large wood projects. It is the primary tool for the majority of woodworking shops. Woodworkers will spend a significant amount of time working on the table saw to cut various aspects of a job. It can perform a range of different cutting techniques and joinery. It is able to perform two primary kinds of cuts: the crosscut and the tear cut. A crosscut happens the cut that is made across the shorter dimension of an object of wood, and an rip cut occurs when you cut across the length of the wood.

Chapter 14: Shop Safety

If you work with cutting saws that could break a limb and large boards It is essential to be cautious and avoid any mistakes that could endanger your health or possibly your entire life!

Goggles or safety glasses should be worn when power tools are used as well as during sculpting, sanding cutting or hitting overhead. This is crucial for anyone who wears contact lenses. Wear ear protection when using high-frequency power tools. Some tools are operating at high the level of sound that can damage hearing.

Clean up loose hair and clothing so that it doesn't get caught in tools. Roll your sleeves and remove jewelry. Keep tools out of reach of children.

A suitable respirator or mask should be worn when sanding, sawing, or using substances that emit toxic fumes. The flammable nature of oily rags is evident from the moment they are used So be cautious when you dispose of and keep them.

Keep blades sharp. A dull blade requires extreme force to hold it and could slip, which causes accidents.

Always use the right tool for the job. Repair or dispose of tools that have cracks in the handles made of wood or chips on the metal components.

Do not drill, cut or cut anything that's not solidly secured. Be careful not to abuse your tools.

Avoid working using tools when you're exhausted. This is when the majority of incidents happen. Avoid working with tools if you've previously been drinking alcohol. Alcohol can alter your judgement. Be sure to wait until you've completed your work! Don't smoke near combustible objects such as the solvents and stains.

Learn the owner's manual for all tools and learn the proper use of them. Remove all power tools from the circuit when changing settings or replacing parts.

Make sure you are careful when the fence settings for table saws and the guidelines for cutting using security guards and push sticks pushing blocks, fencing straddlers or feather board.

The most efficient tool in your toolbox is your mind Use it. Making your cuts and movements through before acting will help you save both fingertips and the scrap of wood. Be aware of your actions. The moment you glance up to watch the TV in the store or a visitors could result in your hands coming into contact to the cutting blade. Always wait until you've finished cutting before taking your eyes off of the blade.

Be aware that this is something to do, and stop when you're feeling overwhelmed or angry when working on a project. We make mistakes when we rush to complete a task. If your saw can't take cuts, take a break it and examine the issue. A rip fence that isn't aligned properly or poor-seated throat plates can often cause a piece of wood to become stuck between cuts. The board being pushed in these situations could trigger an ejector or even collision with blade. It is important to take a moment to look over the situation and pinpoint the problem.

Stop the machine from running. Allowing the power tool to unwind following a cut is a common security blunder. Even without power, the rotating blade is still able to cause some destruction.

Accidents can be caused through negligence, taking risks or relying on poor judgment, fatigue as well as the horseplay. Other causes include poor guidelines (not studying handbooks) not using guards, inappropriate clothing and equipment, a malfunctioning device, a poor working space, and inadequate lighting.

The most important step to avoid accidents is to familiarize yourself with the new device before using it. Before you do that, go through the instruction manual or do a dry run using the device disconnected. Use the device or tool for its intended purpose.

If it's an two-person task Don't try to complete the task on your own. Make sure you wait until help is provided.

Keep a tidy store. A messy shop can be a disaster that is waiting to happen. Maintaining your store in order can help in protecting you along with your gear from risk. Define the location where hand tools are stored and sort screws, nails and other tools into containers. Make sure to clean up at the close each day. Dust and solvent fumes could pose hazards to health and explosives. Be sure to ensure that there is fresh air, and only use vent fans that are safe from explosions.

While there are certain safety guidelines you should be following, it helps when you know the most frequent mistakes newbies make when they begin their woodworking projects.

Chapter 15: Woodworking Hand Tools And Machinery

HAND TOOL FOR WOODWORKING

Being familiar with frequently used tools and equipment for woodworking is the most important step that can ensure security and efficiency. There are many types, however below is a brief overview of only the most common:

Saws

We offer a variety of sawing tools. These include:

Chainsaw

It is a mobile mechanical saw. It is equipped with teeth in a chain that run through the guide bar. It is utilized for tree felling , bucking as well as for the limping process, the felling of snags and pruning, and for taking firewood for harvesting. A different type of chainsaw are able to be used for more difficult tasks like cutting concrete , or cutting ice. Anyone who is using these types of equipment is known as a sawyer.

Jigsaw

A jigsaw is an instrument used to cut bends that are subjective like stenciled plans , or other customized designs, into pieces of metal, wood or any other material. It is often used in an innovative style that is different from other saws that typically cut straight lines. This is similar to an etch and grate. Although it is possible to use a jigsaw to cut off arbitrary examples cutting straight is more challenging.

Then, he saw

It could be a kind of saw in which the cutting motion is achieved via a push. In addition, it produces an action from the steel that has been sharpened.

Circular saw

A Circular saw or force saw made of an untoothed or rough circular steel or sharpened to break down different materials through a turning motion when it rotates about an arbor. A ring and opening saw also make use of a turning motion, but they aren't identical to the Circular saw. They could also be employed to sharpen steel. Circular saws were developed in the latter half of the 18th century, and were similar in terms of their method of usage.

Different kinds of Circular saws include; Roll joiner , Grating Saw, Carbide saws, Brush cutter, Solid Saw, Cool saw, Miter Saw (hack saw or cut-off) and Flip-over saws (the combination of the compound Miter saw and Table Saw) board saw, multi-device (power tool) Outspread armsaw pendulum saw, the swing saw, Table saw, and the Sally saw.

Miter Saw

The basic miter saw is going to become a manually operated miter. The saw is suspended on rollers that slide in a series with a clinched metal aide, which is fitted by using the miter box. This allows precise crosscuts, and you can also cut miter cuts. These are used frequently, for instance, for picture encircling, or by woodworking enthusiasts who are manual.

Planes

The various kinds of planes are:

Hand Plane

A hand woodworking planer is a tool for modeling wood. When powered with a lot of power, the device could be referred to as a planer. Planes are employed to smooth out, reducing the amount of and give the open with a smooth surface, reducing the unpleasant sound of woods or tone. Planes can be used to create straight, vertical or slanted levels on the workpiece usually, but not always too big to be used for molding. The most exceptional types of planning machines are made to cut joints or enhance moldings.

Molding Plane

A molding plane is a particular plane that is used to make the fascinating shapes you see in wood moldings.

Block Plane

Block carpenter's plan is a hand plane for woodworking that typically features the bottom of the iron at an angle lower than other planes, and the bevel raised. It is made to cut caryopsis at the end and is generally compact enough to be operated using just only one hand.

Chisel

A chisel is a tool that has a distinct, curved cutting edge made of steel that has been sharpened on its end, to cut or cutting hard materials such as stone, wood or even metal with a hand, hitting using a hammer, or with mechanical force. The handle and razor-sharp edge of various kinds of etch are constructed of wood or made of metal that has sharp edges.

Carpentry chisels can range from tiny hand instruments to create minor elements to huge chisels that are employed to remove huge sections of wood in roughing out the condition of an example or a configuration. Typically, when woodcarving, you begin with a larger tool, then gradually moves to smaller instruments to finish the area of the most interest.

Tools for measuring and marking

Instruments for measuring and marking play the most important part in accurate carpentry. Make sure you measure twice, and you'll only need to cut one time especially when you have these instruments near to. These tools include; Level of the bull's eye, Calipers to measure chalk line Coggeshall slide ruler, Combination square, laser Line Level,

Marking Gauge marker knife, moisture Meter plub bob, ruler Scratch awl T bevel speed squares, spirit level Square of steel, Storey pole Straightedge, Tape Measure, Try a square and a Winding stick. And the marking Tools comprise: Scratch Awl, Scriber marking knife wood scribe.

Tools for striking

A vast array of striking tools are typically employed for woodworking tasks. They are available in various layouts and complicated specifications. They include ball pen claw hammer, hammer the sledge hammer, stoning hammer machine hammer, mallet faces made of plastic, for example. They are made of hardened steel and are tempered.

Clamps and clamps

In the beginning, it is important to understand there's a distinction between the two types of clamps. A clamp is a device constructed of metal or wood that has a screw on one end. It's designed to hold pieces of wood securely and stop moving until the glue sets while a cramp is metal piece that has been bent at the ends, used to hold pieces of stone, timber or other materials.

Work-bench and Work-supports

Work supports and, in particular, the work-bench are usually table used by woodworkers to transport workpieces while they work using other techniques. There are a variety of wooden benches and supports, all of which reflect the task to be finished or the technique used by the craftsman working. A majority of benches have two characteristics that they share: they are robust and heavy enough to remain in place while the wood is being constructed, and some method of holding the work in the right height and in a comfortable place so that the worker is able to work with both hands working with the tools. The most important distinction between benches is the method by the way that their workpieces are held. The majority of benches come with a variety of ways of doing this according to the process that is being carried out.

Drills

A drill is an instrument equipped with sharp edges, or with a pointed edge to drill holes into tough materials, often with a rotary abrasion, or repeated blows. Drills are typically employed in woodworking. Hand drills are examples of; Bow drill, Brace and bit, Gimlet, Breast drill Hand drill, the push drill. Bits, or more commonly referred to as drill bits however, are cutting tools that are used to create circular holes that have a circular cross-section. Drill bits typically come in a variety of sizes and serve numerous applications. Drill bits are usually attached to a specific mechanism , which is referred to simply as a drill. This rotates them , and delivers the torque and force needed to make the hole.

Equipment for grinding and sharpening

Sharpening and grinding can be an enormous practice with a wide range of woodwork. It could result in extremely good coatings as well as precise measurements. Sharpening is accomplished by cutting away material from the carry out using an abrasive substance that is more challenging than the material used in the carry out, incorporated periodically by means of operations to sharpen the surface to improve smoothness to allow tiny deformations of the hardware without regrinding.

Mallet

Mallets are similar as hammers in the sense that they're nearly identical , but with a bigger head than the one used in hammers. They also serve for delivering an impact. The difference between it and a hammer is that they aren't able to damage the object being struck as like hammers do, so they're great for pounding wood into position.

The mallets head is made out of wood or rubber and does not contain metal so that it does not cause damage to the material that you're working on, making it an ideal hand tool for molding materials.

Spoke Shaves

Spoke shaves are an instrument that is used to smooth and shape wooden shafts and rods. Spoke shaves could contain some or all of the sharpened notches through the shaft of wood pulled to cut it down to the appropriate size. It is also a great tool to create kayak or canoe paddles.

Files and rasps

They are utilized to shape wood. It's made up in the tips, an extended steel bar, then the heel or bottom and then the tang. The tang is connected to a handle, which is generally made from plastic or wood. The bar is composed of sharp teeth. The rasps are usually more awkward to cut than files.

In woodworking, rasps are utilized for quickly removing wood from surfaces that are curved. They can remove less wood than draw knives which makes them easy to take charge of. However, rasps leave rough finishes. The cut-away areas can be easily smoothed using hand tools that are more precise, such as the file.

Burnishes and scrapers

These tools are utilized to polish wood. The process of burning does not shield the wood as a varnish, but it can give it a shiny sheen. Scrappers Scrapper is an woodworking shaping and finishing hand tool. It can be employed to take small quantities of material. It is a great hand tool for difficult grain zones where hand planes could break. Scrapers for cards are ideal to be used on hard woods and are an alternative of Sandpaper. Scraping typically creates a cleaner surface than sanding. It does not block your wood's pores with dirt or dust and does not create the wood with a blur of worn fibers, as the top abrasives.

Woodworking Machines

Saws

Table Saw

A table saw, also called a saw bench is generally an instrument for woodworking that has circular saw blades which is mounted on an arbor. It is powered with an electrical motor, either via belts, directly or through gears. The blade is protruding from the table's top and provides support to the material, typically wood that is to be cut.

Band Saw

The band saw a robust machine that uses an edge made of a continuous metal band with razor-sharp teeth on one side to cut a variety of pieces of woodwork. The band is mounted on two wheels that rotate in the same direction. Certain band saws come with the option of having three or more wheels. Band sawing results in a smooth and uniform cut. This is because it uses an equally distributed load on the teeth. They are especially useful for cutting irregular or curving shapes, however they can also make straight cuts. The minimum diameter of curve that could be cut with a specific saw will be determined by the size of the band made of metal and the kerfs.

Jointer

Jointers solve the problem of being able to work rough lumber. It makes lumber that is fully ready for work. It ensures that the lumber is straight, square, and flat.

Thickness Planer

The thickness plane, commonly referred to as a thicker or an aplaner is a piece of woodworking equipment that can cut boards to a uniform thickness along their length and to flattening equally-sized surface. A thickness planeer could be an essential tool for boards to be smoothed and flat.

Conclusion

For the beginner, woodworking may seem like a difficult and challenging job. However, once you've made your first piece of wood and you'll see that it's not that difficult to do. This is a step-by procedure for building the woodworking product.

www.ingramcontent.com/pod-product-compliance
Lightning Source LLC
Chambersburg PA
CBHW071844080526
44589CB00012B/1108